# About the Author

Richard was born in the town of Fleet in the county of Hampshire in southern England and spent his early childhood in Simon's Town outside Cape Town in South Africa. After school in South Africa, he was a student at two boarding schools in England before attending Britannia Royal Naval College, Dartmouth - the Royal Navy's equivalent of the US Naval Academy in Annapolis Maryland.

After receiving his commission as a Naval Officer in the Royal Navy and serving in the Fishery Protection Squadron, he was appointed as a Navigator and the Meteorologist on the Royal Yacht Britannia for Her Majesty the Queen's Royal Tour of Fiji, New Zealand and Australia before receiving his Wings with the Royal Navy. He flew as a pilot onboard two Royal Navy aircraft carriers operating in the Far East over a four year period with time also spent operating from shore bases in Singapore, Hong Kong, Malaysia and Western Australia.

He was then sent to fly with the US Navy during the Vietnam era and was a member of the first staff of the Navy Fighter Weapons School (Top Gun) in San Diego California. After a final two year aircraft carrier tour with the Royal Navy in the Mediterranean and the Eastern Atlantic, he retired as a Lieutenant Commander RN after 15 years of service and became an international airline pilot with British Overseas Airways Corporation (BOAC) flying to many countries throughout the world.

Taking early retirement from BOAC, he flew with St Lucia Airways in the Caribbean before working for two years in industrial distribution in Indiana. He was subsequently hired as an International Aviation Reinsurance Broker in New York and worked in that industry for over 25 years. He also continued flying as a fighter pilot with the Royal Naval Reserve (Air) Branch for a further 12 years in Europe.

About 20 years ago, he became an ardent peace activist and joined the Coalition for Peace Action in Princeton, New Jersey, and has been a Quaker for a number of years. He is now very active in the name of Peace worldwide and works continuously to reduce US militarism and the death and destruction which is being carried out by the USA, and other countries, around the world.

He is an ardent preservationist and historian and has led historical walking tours in both Cranbury and Princeton in New Jersey for their respective Historical Societies. He also gives talks on many subjects, including New Jersey and the Revolutionary War, Alexander Hamilton and the Marquis de Lafayette - plus on his time living in France and Peace and Quakerism and on topics such as his volunteer work in a variety of countries. He also tutors geography, history and essay writing in the adult education programs at two NGOs in Trenton, New Jersey..

His volunteering abroad has included teaching in the Peruvian Andes and in the Black Townships in Cape Town and working in a Syrian Refugee Camp in Greece and he has spent time with his sponsored families and in their schools in El Salvador, Nicaragua and Bolivia. In addition to these three countries, he has also sponsored families in Mali, Senegal, Nepal, Colombia and the Philippines.

He has lived in five countries - most recently in France for 10 months - and has visited over 130 countries overall. Richard has dual nationality - British and American - and considers himself to be a Global Citizen.

TO: PETER & KATHY,

WITH MANY THANKS FOR ALL

YOUR FRIENDSHIP.

*Richard*

# FLYING THROUGH LIFE

## From Fighter Pilot to Peace Activist

### by Richard Moody

Front Cover

F4K Phantom on the catapult of the Royal Navy aircraft carrier HMS Ark Royal above the Peace Symbol and the Dove of Peace.

**DORRANCE**
PUBLISHING CO
EST. 1920
PITTSBURGH, PENNSYLVANIA 15238

Dorrance Publishing Co
585 Alpha Drive
Pittsburgh, PA 15238
Visit our website at *www.dorrancebookstore.com*

ISBN: 978-1-6495-7223-3
eISBN: 978-1-6495-7731-3

# Contents

# Foreword

I am pleased and honored to write this forward for Richard Moody's book about his conversion from fighter pilot to peace activist. My life journey had significant parallels with Richard's, except my conversion came much earlier in my life.

Richard first became involved with the Coalition for Peace Action (CFPA), where I have served as Executive Director since 1981, in the lead up to the Iraq War in late 2002 and early 2003. He played a key role in exposing a major hole in then Secretary of State Colin Powell's pro-war presentation to the UN Security Council.

He drew on his expertise on military aircraft to show that Iraq did not actually have the fighter aircraft that Powell alleged it did. Unfortunately, when he wrote a letter to the NY Times about this, they refused to publish it. It was later exposed that key Times journalists had bought the false narrative that Powell and others in the George W. Bush Administration promulgated.

Richard's involvement continued as he participated in multiple demonstrations against the Iraq War after it started in March 2003.

Richard was not among the many who rallied around the flag and switched to support the war once it started. It was especially important for military veterans like Richard to be involved as key supporters of the anti-Iraq war effort. A key slogan we used was "Support our Troops, Bring them Home," and it really helped to have Richard and other veterans give credibility to that message

The CFPA engaged in numerous lobby visits to elected officials from our region and often included Richard in our delegation as he added major credibility to our advocacy. We also included Richard in delegations that did candidate briefings for major party candidates in our region running for Congress.

With the support of Richard and many other veterans, the public awakened to the truth that the American people were misled into the Iraq War, which was a "war of mass deception."

Richard became a member of CFPA in 2004 and has remained one ever since. He has given numerous talks for us, at public rallies and at other events. He is a regular attendee at our Advocacy and Peace Education Committees and also deepened his spiritual grounding in peacemaking by becoming a Quaker.

Richard has become a great personal friend and has made remarkable contributions to our peacemaking efforts. Most recently, he has become our "resident expert" on drone warfare and has composed and updated fact sheets on this latest manifestation of militarism and its perils for CFPA's Interfaith Network on Drone Warfare project.

The Rev. Robert Moore
Executive Director, Coalition for Peace Action, headquartered in Princeton, New Jersey, USA

# Chapter 1

## Admiralty House - Simon's Town, South Africa

In 1946, my father, Admiral Sir Clement Moody KCB CB, was appointed Commander-in-Chief South Atlantic and South America Station by the Royal Navy and my family and I boarded the SS Umtali in Southampton on the English Channel for the long voyage to Cape Town. In addition to my sister, Rachel, aged nine, and myself, aged five, my parents brought along our nanny, Shoonie, to keep us under control and to look after us once we had settled into the Admiral's residence - Admiralty House - in Simon's Town on False Bay down the coast from Cape Town. Shoonie did not last long in South Africa and was sent back to England in disgrace for reasons that were never revealed to us youngsters. She was replaced by Ollie and then by Jo who eventually sailed with us back to England after our time in South Africa.

It must have been quite a thrill for all of us to be leaving post-war England for the Cape and to discover upon arrival the beauty of the magnificent house, built in 1743 by the Dutch, with its grandiose architecture, its sweeping lawns, its vast vegetable garden across the road and its private beach below the house.

Since I was aged five, my memories of war torn England, which we had just left, are understandably cloudy but I do remember the excitement of drinking hot chocolate while hiding under the stairs as German bombers, with their familiar drone, passed overhead and a B17 USAF bomber crashing in flames at a nearby air base after returning from a raid on Germany. There was also the time that the motor of a V1 - the dreaded "doodlebug" flying bomb -

cut out over our house in Hampshire with the V1 coming down in a nearby field - luckily not exploding.

Simon's Town was a new world for all of us - a world without rationing and shortages and long food lines - and a haven for our father after the horrors of his war with the Japanese in the Far East. My father's position brought with it many perks and excesses by today's standards and I suppose I didn't know in my innocence that not everyone was fortunate enough to have twenty five Royal Naval stewards and over twenty gardeners led by the redoubtable Mr Endean.

Looking back on those days of long ago, it's hard to distinguish true personal memories from the stories that my parents related over the subsequent years and also from the photos in our two albums from that time. Photos which include one of me astride one of the ancient cannons on the lawn at Admiralty House and one of Admiralty House itself which hung in our parents' drawing room (living room) in our house in Hampshire in southern England for many years.

Whatever the sources, I can still recall many events to this day. Such as being driven to Miss Kemp's School in Kalk Bay by Corporal Kells, Royal Marines, in our Rover which had been shipped from England, together with three other officers' children. One of whom sadly died in middle age after a distinguished career in the Foreign Office where he held a number of Ambassadorships. Another school friend was rescued from drowning in False Bay by my sister after school one day.

In addition to learning Afrikaans at school, which was sadly soon forgotten, I remember when my father's personal driver, Sergeant Paris, would occasionally drive us to school in the official Admiral's Buick which was permanently positioned at Admiralty House. As if being chauffeur driven to school by a Marine Corporal in a Rover wasn't a treat in itself.

Other recollections, in no particular order, are eating "donna pips", the seeds from fir cones, that fell from a large pine tree at the bottom of the lawn, walking up the many steps on Klava, the mountain behind the house, with my mother and my claiming that a puff adder had winked at me on the way down. And baboons frequently coming down from Klava to raid the kitchen and the days when the irrigation sluice gates in the large vegetable garden were opened and water poured down the man made channels to water the rows of vegetables.

There was also the day that the Dutch aircraft carrier, the Karel Doorman, put to sea with much excitement and the afternoon that I appeared naked from our private beach and burst in on a formal garden party being held on the lawn. Our beach had a shark net strung from the end of the pier to the shore but I never did understand how it worked since the bottom of the net was a mere two feet below the surface. There were also train rides to Muizenberg and on to Cape Town from the station just beyond the bottom of the garden.

I learned to ride my bike on the lawns of Admiralty House - aided by the slope in the middle which helped me launch myself on my first solo. My biking tutor was Chief Petty Officer Parsons, my father's Coxswain of the Admiral's Barge, who coincidentally was there to greet me when I showed up some thirteen years later at Britannia Royal Naval College Dartmouth (BRNC) - the Royal Navy's equivalent of the US Naval Academy (USNA) in Annapolis Maryland. I also experienced my first aerial ride when I rode with my father to Bloemfontein in a two engine piston and suffered from excruciating earache in this non-pressurised aircraft.

I also remember my sister once admonishing my mother for calling one of the stewards "darling", which was of course his last name, and my parents entertaining many distinguished visitors including Tyrone Power, the American actor, Joe Davis, the English snooker player, Issy Bloomberg, the Mayor of Cape Town and Lord Montgomery of El Alamein who presented my parents with a fine photo of himself in battledress the day he crossed the Rhine in 1944. There was also a photo of Monty with my parents on the steps at Admiralty House which hangs in our house in Cranbury New Jersey. Issy Bloomberg subsequently invited me to horse racing at Milnerton (now a training center) when I returned to the Cape for the first time twenty years later.

The biggest excitement must have been the visit of King George VI and Queen Elizabeth and the two young Princesses, Elizabeth and Margaret, when they sailed from England to Cape Town in the battleship HMS Vanguard. The drive-in porch (a porte cochere) had to be widened to accommodate the Royal Buick, a golden spade for tree planting purchased and preparations made for many guests to be presented to the King and Queen on the lawn.

A tree was duly planted by the King with the golden spade and Margaret cheekily saying she hoped that the spade would not be hung above her father's bed with the risk of falling and braining him in the night. When the King and

Queen departed by train to Pretoria, the King asked my mother "How do you like me (sic!) new suit?"

Sadly, my halcyon days in Simon's Town eventually came to an end and I sailed back to boarding school in England on board the SS Stirling Castle leaving me with wonderful memories of Simon's Town and the Cape.

I was back in the Cape with my wife, Lisa, when we taught in the Black Townships to the east of Cape Town and we were fortunate to be granted access to Admiralty House where I was reunited with my old bedroom and given the chance to again explore the lovely gardens where I had learned to ride my bike and the beach where I had learned to swim. Admiralty House is now the residence of a senior Admiral in the South African Navy and it still looks very much the way it did all those years ago.

# Chapter 2

## Growing Up in England in the 1950s

---

The small town of Fleet in the county of Hampshire in southern England takes its name from the Anglo Saxon word "Flete" which meant a large body of water since there is still a lake on th edge of town - a lake which was drained during World War II (WWII) as it was a conspicuous landmark for German bombers attempting to destroy the airfield at the nearby Royal Aircraft Establishment at Farnborough.

I spent my childhood in the 50s in this attractive town which sits about forty miles southwest of London on the main railway line between the City's Waterloo Station and Southampton on the English Channel. Fleet grew in population with the expansions of the railway network and the military garrison at Aldershot, about five miles away, and, after WWII, it became a dormitory town for London with its easy ride by train for commuters working in "Smoke" as the big city was unfortunately called due to the prevailing smog.

My family and I lived in a five bedroom house built in the 1920s on two acres of land about one mile from the town centre and the house, by today's standards, would be deemed to have been very poorly equipped since it only had one bathroom with a tub but no shower. The house was inefficiently heated by hot water filled radiators with the heat for the water being provided by a coal fired boiler in the kitchen. The bedrooms also had small electric fired heaters which were essential after the normally almost cold baths as the bath water was merely warmed by an inefficient little electric heater called an Ascot.

Apart from a large kitchen, there was a central dining room, a drawing room, a schoolroom (a recreation room) and a lovely veranda which led out onto the lawn. The garden was, and still is, quite idyllic with its large lawn leading down to a vista cut through the trees. On one side of the vista was a large vegetable garden and, on the other side, a chicken coop and a run for the hens which many families kept in post war Britain due to rationing. Sadly one night, all the hens did not survive a marauding badger - or perhaps it was a fox. Rationing lasted into the early 50s and was then introduced again in 1956 during the Suez Crisis with Egypt. There was also a delightful herbaceous border of flowers running down the left side of the lawn and a brick pergola with roses which my father had built in his retirement from the Royal Navy.

Everybody had servants in those days and they, and delivery men, would only come to the back door of the house via the Tradesman's Entrance. Bottled milk was delivered daily by the milkman from his electric float and personally deposited by him on the doorstep at the back door and the wonderful Mr Silver would cycle down to our house from his Cane's grocery shop in town once a week to jot down my mother's weekly shopping list of required items from his store. I have vivid memories of him showing up in his long trousers with bicycle clips around his ankles and sitting at the kitchen table with a cup of tea and his notebook and pencil in hand as my mother went through the list of mainly dried goods she needed that week. The next day dear old Mr Silver would come drifting back in his little van and deliver the goods - always of course through the Tradesman's Entrance. There was also a very tame tiny robin redbreast who seemed to know when Mr Silver was coming and would hop through the often open window onto the kitchen table hoping Mr Silver might have brought a tidbit for him from his shop.

There were my parents cleaning lady - Mrs Godwin - who came every day to clean the house and make the beds and Ethel who came once a week and was more of a scullery maid than a cleaner. The house had a pantry for the silverware and dishes, a scullery for the heavy duty pots and pans and a larder where most of the foodstuffs that needed to be cooled were kept. There was a small fridge but no freezer so I imagine we didn't keep perishable foods for very long. There was also an attached coal shed by the back door into which the coalman would dump our purchased coal on a regular basis.

Why Mrs G was not called by her first name, Mary, was never explained to me and yet Ethel was always Ethel and nobody thought that was strange. Mrs G acknowledged my mother with a grunting sound which I think was her way of saying "Madam" - the title that Ethel always used.

There was also Charlie, the Maltese gardener and serious racing road cyclist who used to take me to watch Aldershot Town play football (soccer) in Division 111 South - about three rungs from the top of what is now known as the Premier League. Aldershot, still playing at an even lower professional level in the National League, were always called The Shots although, when they were losing, Charlie was prone to call them by the more demeaning name of The Sh*ts and was sometimes known to yell "The Shots give me the Sh*ts"!

Charlie was fired when my mother came back from a month's vacation in Spain to find that he had not shown up for work and yet she had paid him in advance. He was replaced by the taciturn Mr Ayres - known simply as Ayres. I never did know his first name and he spent a lot of time wandering into the kitchen looking for a cup of tea from my mother.

My mother, Lady Moody, had worked serving food in a canteen at the railway station for soldiers during the War and was a reasonable cook - if you can call such as Bubble and Squeak, Toad in the Hole, Kedgeree, Kippers and Shepherd's Pie (always lamb of course) etc as reasonable food. Apart from two pubs in town, I can't recollect any restaurants besides Mrs Lunn's Tea Room and we always ate meals at home and there was no such thing as fast or take out food.

After retiring from the Royal Navy as a Vice Admiral, my father joined the local Police Constabulary at the lowest rank - Special Constable - and rode around town in uniform on his bike - of course, unarmed - and was the go-to man for anyone needing advice or directions. Inviting an enquirer into the Police Station for a cup of tea, my father would provide the necessary answers and then send the satisfied individual on his or her way.

My father was also Chairman of the Urban District Council (similar to a US town's present day Mayor) and the equivalent of the Town Hall is still named after him. Being an ardent cricket fan, he would often travel to Kennington Oval in London with Mr Baker, who owned the local ironmongery (hardware store), to see England or Surrey in action. My father sadly died at age 69 from a heart attack while drinking a Gin and Tonic in the local pub,

The Oatsheaf. He had fought at Gallipoli in the Great War and experienced the suicidal Japanese kamikaze attacks on his aircraft carrier during the War in the Pacific and the stress and horrors of combat finally caught up with him. Every time I return to Fleet, I have a Gin and Tonic in his honour at the much improved Oatsheaf.

Fleet still has an excellent golf club called the North Hants GC where I was given lessons by the pro - Mr Mounce - and it was later at this club that Justin Rose of subsequent PGA fame learned his golf - being sponsored as a young lad by the father of a friend of mine who ran the Golf Foundation Society.

Another popular sport - long a relic of the past - was Cycle Speedway where teams of two cyclists in each team rode against each other around an oval track on their bicycles. Our team was known as the Fleet Falcons and they competed against teams from nearby towns such as the Cobham Rockets and the Elstead Vampires and cycle speedway vied with cricket and football for popularity in town.

As was mentioned earlier, smog was a massive problem in post war England and I remember one day being asked by the bus driver on the bus to Aldershot to walk in front of his bus with a large torch (flashlight) to light up the road as the visibility was next to zero.

With my current aversion to the fire sirens which are still used in a number of US communities, I must admit that I and my best friend would leap on our bikes at the sound of the local siren, peddle like mad to the Fire Station to find out the fire's location and then frantically dashing to the scene of action before the fire was extinguished. Afterwards, the friendly firemen would often hoist our bikes on to their fire truck, offer us seats in the cabin and drive us back to town.

I cannot remember any crime at all in Fleet and the most sensational event of my childhood was when a certain Mrs Mellor rolled her car on a bend after taking her husband to the railway station for his daily commute to London. It was not the accident that shocked everyone but the fact she was only wearing her nightie. Oh, the innocence of those days.

Religion was low key with the majority of churchgoers being Church of England. I reluctantly was taken to church on some Sundays and, being extremely bored by one lengthy prayer, I decided, while kneeling, to stick my head through one of the open backed chairs in front of me which the church used instead of pews. Unfortunately, my head got stuck and my embarrassed father had to haul me out of church with the chair stuck to my head.

Fleet hasn't changed much in the ensuing years. It now has a larger population and more traffic, a supermarket and fewer family owned shops and it's still a dormitory town for London and a home for many Army officers based in Aldershot. I wonder if Mrs Lunn's Tea Room is still there? The Oatsheaf certainly is and what a fine watering hole it has now become compared to the rather dingy pub it was all those years ago. As you can see, tea featured very prominently many moons ago and it still does - life hasn't really changed in rural England. As the Great War poet, Rupert Brooke, once wrote - "Oh yet stands the church clock at ten to three and is there honey still for tea?".

# Chapter 3

## The Fishery Protection Squadron

The Fishery Protection Squadron - colloquially known as the "Fish Squadron" - was reputed to be the oldest seagoing Squadron in the Royal Navy. Horatio Nelson once served as Captain of HMS Albemarle in this Squadron during his distinguished career with the Royal Navy which ended with his death, as Admiral Lord Nelson, at the Battle of Trafalgar against the French and Spanish fleets in 1805.

The Fish Squadron's role was always to protect the fishing rights of the British Isles by patrolling the waters around this island nation and also to support British fisherman fishing in international waters. My first job after being commissioned as an Acting Sub Lieutenant was in the Fish Squadron in the 1960s where the protection of the British Isles was carried out by my Home Division which attempted to prevent foreign fishing vessels from poaching inside UK territorial limits. These limits were originally out to three miles offshore but more recently were extended to twelve miles. There was also the Channel Division, comprising small inshore minesweepers, which patrolled the English Channel - mainly in search of French poachers.

The expanded role to protect British fishing vessels, mainly trawlers, who were fishing further afield in waters such as those surrounding Iceland, Norway, the Faeroes, Greenland, the White Sea and the Barents Sea, was carried out by the larger frigates of the Arctic Division. An undeclared "Cod War" took place with Iceland from the 1950s to the 1970s with Icelandic gunboats at times firing on mainly Scottish trawlers - in particular one ironically called the Red Crusader - who were illegally fishing within the territorial limits of Iceland. Iceland expanded its limits from four miles to twelve miles to fifty miles to two hundred miles over a number of years after Iceland declared an Exclusive Economic Zone (EEZ). Many international incidents occurred between Great Britain and Iceland involving the Arctic Division of long range frigates but no actual war was ever fought. Since Brexit came into play, fishing rights have become front and centre with Britain's continuing disagreements with the European Union.

After Britannia Royal Naval College (BRNC), always known as Dartmouth due to its location in the harbour of that name in Devonshire, I was appointed to be the Navigator and Fishery Officer of a coastal minesweeper in the Home Division of the Fish Squadron. The term minesweeper is misleading as our actual role was to patrol the waters of the United Kingdom and we only once used our minesweeping gear - in a NATO exercise out of Ijmuiden in Holland.

My coastal minesweeper, HMS Wotton, one of many named after villages ending in "ton", was based at Port Edgar on the Firth of Forth near Edinburgh in Scotland. Port Edgar was a "Stone Frigate", named HMS Lochinvar, since the base was not a seagoing vessel but a small shore-based naval port. The Senior Officer of the entire Fish Squadron - known as "Captain Fish" - was stationed there and I remember that HMS Lochinvar's First Lieutenant - the base's second in command - used to ride to work on horseback.

HMS Wotton was 400 tons displacement and 150 feet long and was powered by two diesel engines with four officers and thirty crew. Wotton's only armament was a 40 mm Bofors gun on the foredeck which we never had to fire in earnest. Uniforms were only worn going in and out of harbour (jeans and foul weather gear being the usual order of the day at sea) and our role was akin to a seagoing gamekeeper in search of sneaky poachers. Our territory included covering the Orkneys and Shetland Islands and Fair Isle to the north of Scotland in addition to the waters of the United Kingdom (UK) but, for light relief and Rest and Recreation (R & R), we also visited Haugesund in Norway (where our ship's soccer eleven, on which I played right wing, lost 12-0 to a local team), Randers - up a fjord in Denmark - and Galway in the west of Ireland. This was in addition to stopovers in many ports around the British Isles.

Those were the days when the UK's territorial limits were three miles offshore with a prohibition on fishing by all foreign nations within those limits. Our poachers were mainly Russians, Poles, Danes, Dutch and French who, if not trawling, were "long lining" or using seine nets.

One notorious Polish poacher used to sneak inside the limit off Suffolk on the east coast of England when he felt the coast was clear. Determined to nab him, we positioned two groups of sailors with radios and sextants - those were the days before Global Positioning Systems (GPS) or Satellite Navigation (SatNav) - at separate positions on the cliffs close to the area where he was known to poach. Meanwhile, Wootton, looking dormant docked in nearby Lowestoft, was in fact at immediate readiness for sail with its diesel engines flashed up. As soon as our teams on the cliffs had fixed the Pole's illegal position with the use of their sextants and had reported to Wotton that our target was inside the limits, our gallant minesweeper swept into action and an apprehension was made.

Being the Fishery Officer, my role on these occasions was to leap into a Gemini rubber dinghy, powered by an outboard motor, with two of the "lads" (as we called the sailors) and carry out an attempted arrest. Surprisingly, no fisticuffs with the arrestees ever occurred although numerous attempts were made to bribe me and my assistants by filling our dinghy with large amounts of flailing cod, haddock, turbot, hake and various other types of seawater fish.

Many of the Scottish fishermen also fished illegally with nets which, being too small, did not conform to the law since they were able to catch young fish which were below the minimum legal size. My job as Fishery Officer was to measure the illegal nets and, after always accepting the boat full of fish as the usual bribe, file a citation which would sometimes result in a financial penalty for the pleading fisherman. One favorite area for illegal fishing was off the mouth of the River Dee on the east coast of Scotland. The Dee is famous for its salmon and many of these expensive and much desired fish were caught with illegally small nets - much to our dismay.

One Frenchman was always illegally fishing inside the limits off Cornwall in southwest England and, after arresting him, the Captain of Wotton and I had to don our little used uniforms and appear in court, with a lawyer known as a Procurator Fiscal, presenting our case to the local Judge. Incidentally, my Captain was a Naval pilot who had flown the Sea Vixen, the fighter I subsequently flew off the aircraft carrier HMS Eagle a few years later. His uncle was a distinguished Army officer who had won the Victoria Cross (VC) - Britain's top military award for gallantry - while serving with the Gloucestershire Regiment (known as the Glorious Glosters) in the Korean War.

One crafty French "long liner" was often sneaking into UK waters off Stornoway in the Scottish Outer Hebridean islands but always at night when the coast appeared to be clear. Fishing boats at night are required to display certain distinguishing lights if they have a long line of nets astern of them which would be a hazard to other shipping. Determined to apprehend him, we too put up trawler lights one night, disguising Wotton as a fishing vessel, and steamed into the illegal area successfully fooling the Frenchman into thinking that we were another trawler poaching inside the limit and therefore the coast must be clear.

My job in my dinghy was to drop a reflective radar buoy in the middle of the Frenchman's circular line so that Wotton's radar could plot where the Frenchman was illegally fishing. Unfortunately, he was cleverer than we were and he succeeded in snagging the radar buoy, known as a Dan buoy, in the loop of his line, pulling the buoy onboard his vessel and thus preventing us from proving that he had been fishing illegally.

The Russian fishing fleets were also a problem with their large groups of trawlers all controlled by a mother ship - a large cargo vessel that acted as a home away from home for the smaller fishing vessels. In addition to poaching, the trawlers and the mother ship were prolific in dumping trash (known as "Ditching Gash" in the Royal Navy) in the North Sea. "Ditching Gash" is now a very serious problem in the world's oceans with vast amounts of plastics and other garbage destroying so much of the sea life.

One particular Russian mother ship was a persistent "gash ditcher" so yours truly was told to head over to it one morning in my motorized rubber dinghy with a chart in hand, climb a rope ladder up the side of the rolling Russian vessel and inform the Russians where they could and could not ditch their gash.

I had studied Russian in high school and at BRNC Dartmouth and was an unofficial Russian Interpreter although my knowledge of the language left a lot to be desired. Much to my surprise, there were women crew members onboard, which was a rare occurrence in those days, and the Russians delighted in plying me with vodka in an attempt to get me to change the subject. Relations were very cordial and I think I did manage to get them to alter their dumping habits. However, the copious amounts of vodka got the better of my grip on the rope ladder when climbing back down to my dinghy from the rolling Russian ship and my precious chart, with all the plotted evidence of the Russian's activities, disappeared forever into the depths of the North Sea.

HMS Wotton was not graced with any luxuries and the two most junior officers (one of them being me) shared a minute cabin with two bunk beds - one above the other. The ship rolled up to 60 degrees either way in rough weather which meant food was scarce since the galley (kitchen) had to partially close down under those conditions and a frequent offering was the easy-to-cook "Chip Butty" which is a quite revolting chip (French fries) sandwich. And all furniture - the little there was - had to be laid on its side for fear of damage if it came crashing down in heavy seas. This often occurred in the North Sea and particularly to the north of Scotland where the full force of the Atlantic rollers would sweep eastwards to collide with our small vessel. The Captain was lucky enough to have his own small cabin - as did his second in command, the First Lieutenant.

My cabin mate had the tedious job of being Supply Officer and Secretary - responsible for the supply of food and equipment and also for writing formal letters. The majority of communication however was carried out with basic telegram messages - or even using hand held flag signalling by semaphore if Wotton was within visual range of another Naval vessel.

The Bridge (where the Officer of the Watch controlled the ship) had no microphone for communication but instead a voice pipe was used to pass orders to the helmsman and engine room artificer - both of whom were on a lower deck. The Bridge was open to the elements which made attempts at coastal navigation extremely difficult in foul weather but my time onboard Wotton did allow me to obtain my Bridge Watchkeeping and my Ocean Navigation Certificates.

The latter involved carrying out the celestial navigation of Wotton by sextant when out of sight of land. This required me to take star sights at nautical twilight at dawn and dusk - plus shots of the sun during the day including one when the sun was at its highest - known as a Meridian Altitude - which determined the ship's latitude.

Naturally, this means of navigation can only be done with clear skies but it did hold me in good stead when I was subsequently appointed to the Royal Yacht Britannia and I managed to navigate the Yacht by sextant across the Atlantic, Pacific and Indian Oceans during the course of the Royal Tours of Fiji, New Zealand and Australia.

For a period of time, we were loaned a wonderful Royal Naval Reserve officer who was a Scottish trawlerman from Peterhead on the northeast coast of Scotland. It took a number of weeks for me to get to understand his broad Scottish brogue but we became lifelong friends and are still in touch all these years later. In those days, Bill owned a small trawler for coastal fishing but, as the years went by, his fishing boats, all named Sundari, grew in size until his last vessel before retirement a few years ago was a vast ocean going trawler as luxurious as a small cruise liner. One of his earlier trawlers capsized in the Atlantic with all the crew surviving and now Bill lives on a seaside Scottish golf course (not one owned by a certain ex President) and enjoys puttering around the course when he's not at the Fishermen's Mission with his long time seagoing mates reminiscing about days gone by.

Life onboard Wotton taught me about survival in tough times, how to navigate across the oceans and seas and to control a Naval vessel in heavy seas and foul weather as Officer of the Watch. And, above all, to take the rough with the smooth and make the most of every opportunity that came my way - including amazingly (and stupidly) swimming in March in the frigid waters of the idyllic Scottish fishing harbor of Ullapool in the Inner Hebrides - and also discovering the delights of Laphroaig Scotch whisky on the island of Islay.

Needless to say, my subsequent service and experiences onboard H.M.Yacht Britannia were a trifle different to the rough and tumble that I had experienced on a coastal minesweeper in the Fishery Protection Squadron.

# Chapter 4

## Round the World on the Queen's Yacht

---

As described in the previous chapter, my first appointment as a very green Naval officer had been the navigator of a small coastal minesweeper in the Fishery Protection Squadron based out of the Firth of Forth near Edinburgh in Scotland. It was therefore to my great surprise that I was summoned for an interview onboard a very different type of ship - Her Majesty the Queen's Royal Yacht Britannia. After the rough and tumble of my Fishery Protection days, I must have been wearing a new uniform, had my hair cut, shaved, kept my nose clean and behaved in an officer-like fashion when placed in front of the Flag Officer Royal Yachts - Rear Admiral Joseph Henley - who was interviewing me for the position of Assistant Navigator and Meteorologist to the Queen.

The Royal Yacht - built in 1953 and now a floating museum near Edinburgh - was the only Royal Navy vessel commanded by an Admiral (not a Captain) and the title "Flag Officer Royal Yachts" stems back to Charles I's days when he had many smaller Yachts at his disposal. It was even more of a surprise when I was awarded the position and I was soon sent to the Royal Naval School of Meteorology in Cornwall in southwest England to learn the world's weather in two weeks. The Yacht was shortly to set sail on a Round the World cruise with Her Majesty, Prince Philip - the Duke of Edinburgh - and the Royal Household subsequently flying out from England for the Royal Tours of Fiji, New Zealand and Australia onboard the Yacht. Here I was, aged twenty one as a young Lieutenant, about to set sail on the most palatial of all vessels on the most exotic tour imaginable with only two weeks worth of knowledge about the complexity of the world's weather and the challenge of navigating this floating palace around the world and across three oceans.

I was the most junior of the twenty officers aboard and my cabin mate, Nick, was in charge of the Royal Barge which took the Royal couple ashore when docking the Yacht alongside a jetty was not feasible. At times with no Royalty onboard, the Barge was also used by our playboy Admiral to water ski with his Australian Flag Lieutenant acting as coxswain.

Nick and I lived in the tiniest of cabins in the bowels of the vessel with no portholes (windows) but at least we didn't have to share a bunk. After service with the Royal Navy, Nick ended up as number two with the United Nations High Commissioner for Refugees seeing service in the Middle East and Balkans before retiring to Scotland having been awarded the Nobel Peace Prize. Our cabin is now a storage locker and, unsurprisingly, is not part of the ship's tour that can be taken onboard by the public.

Life on the Yacht was very gentlemanly and tranquil with no loudspeaker announcements and we sailed from England and visited the Azores, Jamaica and Balboa in Panama before passing through the Panama Canal and on to Tahiti and the tiny Pacific island of Palmerston before arriving in Fiji to await the Royal Family who were to spend the next two months on board. I particularly remember the Azores as I surprisingly shot a blind eagle two in total fog on a mountain golf course where I never once saw the flag stick until walking onto the par four green. I still have my scorecard to prove it.

Nick and I each had our own steward, Steward Neale - a far cry from life on my minesweeper - and at lunch in harbour our steward would ask us what sporting and civilian clothes we would be wearing that afternoon as golf, tennis and socialising were often the order of the day. Sure enough, our requested clothing would be laid out on our bunks when we returned to our cabin after lunch.

After taking the Queen and her entourage around Fiji, we transported the Royals to New Zealand and visited many ports and cities on both North and South Island, including Auckland and Wellington, before heading across the Tasman Sea to Adelaide in South Australia. This was followed by a counter clockwise cruise around Australia visiting all the major coastal cities and towns, plus visits to Hayman Island and Green Island near the Great Barrier Reef. We also stopped in Broome and Geraldton and some of the more isolated communities on the northwestern and western coasts of Australia before the Royals flew back to England from Perth in Western Australia. But not before the Queen had knighted our Admiral - now Admiral Sir Joseph Henley KCVO (Knight Commander of the Victorian Order) - on the quarterdeck of the Royal Yacht.

On our way out to the Antipodes, Admiral Henley had become enamoured with an attractive American lady in Jamaica and the year after his knighthood he was back in Jamaica - still in command of the Royal Yacht - when he conveyed Princess Margaret, the Queen's younger sister, on her honeymoon to the Caribbean. The Anglo/American "liaison" blossomed and the Admiral subsequently divorced Lady Henley and married his American heartthrob - only to be dismissed as Flag Officer Royal Yachts since, in those days, the Royal Family saw divorce as quite unacceptable. How times have changed.

In harbour, my role involved being present at all of the Royal events including horse racing at Flemington (home of the Melbourne Cup) and the many garden parties and social gatherings plus showing V.I.P.s around the Yacht which included a visit to the immaculately clean Engine Room which actually did have a Golden Rivet. But that's a nautical story for another day.

At sea, my life was more frenetic since I carried out all the ocean navigation the old fashioned way - with a sextant - across the Atlantic, Pacific and Indian Oceans, taking shots of the stars at morning and evening nautical twilight and the sun around midday. In the Indian Ocean, I was once able to take sextant shots of the Sun, the Moon and Venus at the same time to establish our position.

My most demanding role was producing the Royal Weather Forecasts which were presented to the Queen on her early morning tea tray on a gold-rimmed embossed card with the title E2R on the top which stood for Elizabeth Regina the Second. A demanding role because those were the days before satellites and plotting the weather map from scratch from an early morning daily coded analysis, known as a CANAL, was an arduous task. My job required drawing up a map of the isobars, fronts, and highs and lows and then attempting to make a forecast with the help of hourly weather reports sent in by other ships in the area - if there were any.

The Admiral would demand to see my weather map before my forecast went to the Queen and one morning I overslept and hurriedly took him a previous day's map with a similar weather pattern, having changed the date, in the hope of fooling the Admiral. Needless to say, he rumbled me and sent me packing.

The other unfortunate event was getting the weather forecast horribly wrong in Wellington New Zealand when a nasty unannounced depression hit this city, which sits on the narrow Cook Strait between North and South Islands. There had been few ships in the Tasman Sea between New Zealand and Australia so I was devoid of other vessels' weather reports and failed to report this serious storm. This left the Yacht unable to dock and the Queen had to go ashore up the coast in the Royal Barge in her mackintosh, rain hat and wellington boots with no red carpet nor receiving party to greet her. Wellington was living up to its name of Windy Wellington.

Once the Royal Household left us in Perth, we had an idyllic sail back to England via Mauritius, Aden in Yemen, the Suez Canal, Malta and Gibraltar with just the officers and sailors (Yachtsmen as the latter were called) enjoying this palatial vessel. In Mauritius, the officers were invited to a dinner party by the British Governor, Sir John Shaw Rennie, at the Governor's Mansion - Le Reduit. Le Reduit was built by the French in 1749 who officially named it Le Chateau du Reduit - reduit meaning citadel or keep in English. After dinner, when the ladies retired to powder their noses, the Governor led us gentlemen into the garden to "water" the ancient roses - a time honoured tradition going back centuries.

When Royalty was onboard at sea, two officers always had dinner with the Royals and so my turn came up from time to time. Sitting next to the Queen, as I did, could have been an intimidating experience but being reasonably knowledgeable on horse racing and breeding and knowing the Queen's love of horses, I was able to keep up my end of the conversation without too many embarrassments.

Prince Philip, being quite the joker, was another matter and he was often playing pranks on the junior officers including dumping my cabin mate, Nick, on his head in the ship's swimming pool, creeping up on me on watch on the navigation bridge in the middle of the night in the Tasman Sea and, having put his hands over my eyes, demanded to know where we were. In New Zealand, he almost closed down a factory by operating a vital switch to test the system - and he subsequently said to an African chieftain who was wearing tribal robes - "You look ready for bed"!

All in all, life on board was very peaceful and efficient and, after arriving back in England after five months away, I was "forced" to attend Royal Ascot, Wimbledon, the Royal Tournament and Garden Parties at Buckingham Palace before we took Queen Elizabeth the Queen Mother on Royal Tours of the Isle of Man and the Channel Islands. Life with the Queen Mum (as she was affectionately known) was very relaxed as she enjoyed her gin and tonics and liked to play the card game called "racing demon" with us young officers when not meeting and greeting ashore.

I was very privileged to have experienced this amazing period in my young life - sandwiched as it was between life onboard a mundane minesweeper and my subsequent pilot's flying training with the Royal Air Force where I lived for ten months in an unheated barrack with certainly no steward to lay out my clothes each day nor the delights of life in the tropics aboard the Queen's personal floating palace.

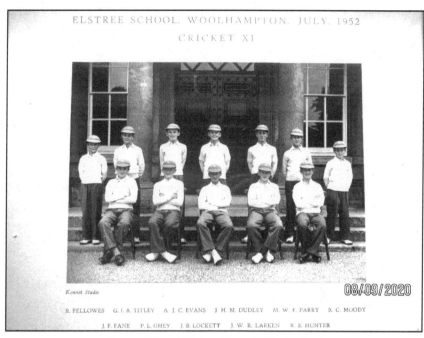

ELSTREE SCHOOL, WOOLHAMPTON, JULY, 1952
CRICKET XI

Kennet Studio

R. FELLOWES    G. I. A. TITLEY    A. J. C. EVANS    J. H. M. DUDLEY    M. W. F. PARRY    R. C. MOODY

J. F. FANE    P. L. GHEY    J. B. LOCKETT    J. W. R. LARKEN    R. S. HUNTER

Elstree School Cricket Team 1952 England

Her Majesty the Queen, Prince Philip and Royal Yacht Officers

H.M. Yacht Britannia off Tahiti

# Chapter 5

## East of Suez

---

After my service in the Royal Yacht, I was sent to Basic Flying Training at the Royal Air Force station RAF Linton on Ouse in Yorkshire in northern England. Earlier, at Britannia Royal Naval College, Dartmouth, in Devon, I had, for some reason, wanted to be a helicopter pilot. In hindsight, I was fortunate to be told that no rotary wing position would be available for me and so I was trained to get my Wings by flying the fixed wing Jet Provost. All ab initio Royal Navy pilots were trained by the RAF and my course was one of the first to solo on jet aircraft with no piston aircraft flying as part of our training.

My father had been a Gunnery Officer and had subsequently commanded an aircraft carrier - HMS Eagle - on the China Station having earlier served in the Gallipoli Campaign in the Dardanelles during the Great War. At Gallipoli, he spent most of his time aloft in a basket hanging underneath a large balloon tethered to what was known as a "Balloon Ship" - in his case HMS Hector - where he controlled the Fleet's naval gunfire onto the Turkish trenches with binoculars and a radio. A "Balloon Ship" was a merchant vessel converted for Naval use with a large hangar on the stern to house the gigantic balloon when it was not in airborne use. These converted ships have since become known as STUFTs - Ships Taken Up From Trade - and many merchant vessels were requisitioned when Britain mounted a counter invasion of the Falkland Islands after the Argentinian takeover in 1982.

In the Dardanelles, my father also flew over enemy territory as an Observer in the back seat of a Henri Farman biplane with the Royal Naval Air Service (RNAS) - again directing naval gunfire and plotting the positions of the Turkish trenches. The RNAS was one of the first military aviation services in the world having been conceived in 1912 and officially commissioned on July 1 1914. I guess flying was in my blood.

After receiving my Wings, I carried out Advanced Flying Training on the Hawker Hunter fighter with the Royal Navy at the Royal Naval Air Station RNAS Brawdy in Pembrokeshire in western Wales and was then sent to RNAS Culdrose in Cornwall and back to Brawdy to convert onto the Fairey Gannet. This, initially, was a disappointment for me as the Gannet was a twin engine carrier based turbo prop and I had had grand visions of being a gung ho jet fighter pilot - which I did subsequently become after a two year tour on Gannets.

The Gannet was an extremely versatile Naval aircraft and its various models carried rockets, bombs, depth charges, torpedoes and mines and was capable of airborne early warning (AEW) and also rocket assisted take off from an aircraft carrier flight deck. It was also very adept at landing on carriers in all weather and deck conditions and, looking back on those far off days, it's still amazing that I got the beast back on board when the deck was frequently heaving and corkscrewing in very poor weather and sea conditions. Many times this was at night and once was on one engine when I suffered an engine fire with no diversionary airfield within 500 miles.

My time on Gannets proved very valuable and set me up nicely for the many deck landings I subsequently carried out in Sea Vixen and F4 Phantom aircraft during two further carrier tours. These latter aircraft were high performance jet fighters whose approach speeds to the carrier were considerably faster than the dear old Gannet. Interestingly, there was one Gannet in the world still flying - in the hands of a collector in New Richmond Wisconsin who endearingly called the old bird Janet the Gannet.

In those days, carrier tours of duty in the Fleet Air Arm - as Naval Aviation continues to be called in the current Royal Navy - were for two years with one year being spent East of Suez. This was a time when Britain still had an Empire (sort of) and deployments to the Far East often involved disembarking the ship's air squadrons to military airfields in such as Singapore, Hong Kong, Nairobi and in northern Malaya near Penang at Royal Australian Airforce (RAAF)

Butterworth. We also used RAF Gan in the Maldive Islands as a diversion airfield and visited the Cocos Islands and Subic Bay in the Philippines. On my first tour East of Suez, we transited the Suez Canal and the Red Sea from and to the Mediterranean with stopovers in Malta and Gibraltar after many operational days in the Indian Ocean and the Far East.

Two highlights of that two year Gannet tour were the Indonesian Confrontation and the Beira Patrol. The former was when Malaya, including Borneo and Singapore, were negotiating independence from Great Britain and the Indonesians attempted to stop this progression through military action in an attempt to take over these countries for themselves. Our carrier, HMS Ark Royal, was one of the Royal Navy warships sent to push back the Indonesians when attempts were made by them to land paratroops on Malayan territory. Whereas most of the heavy fighting was carried out by the Royal Marines and Army on the island of Borneo, I flew numerous patrols to try and prevent any Indonesian paratroopers landing on the Malayan mainland and one night I was shot at when we got too close to the Indonesian island of Sumatra.

During my time East of Suez, Ian Smith, the Prime Minister of Rhodesia (now Zimbabwe), had made a Unilateral Declaration of Independence (UDI) in an attempt to achieve white Rhodesian independence from Britain and sanctions were imposed on Rhodesia. These included the import of oil and, in order to circumvent this restriction, Smith persuaded Mozambique to allow foreign ocean going tankers to transport oil to the port of Beira on the Indian Ocean where the oil would then be shipped by rail across Mozambique and into Rhodesia. Britain had wanted black majority rule in Rhodesia which Smith's minority white party bitterly opposed and so HMS Ark Royal with our squadrons of Sea Vixen, Scimitar and Gannet aircraft was sent to patrol the Mozambique Channel to stop any tankers from reaching Beira during what became known as the Beira Patrol. Very few shots were fired but many tankers were turned away and lengthy sorties were flown. Landing back on board the carrier with no diversion airfield in horrendous sea conditions and heavy swells tested the best of us with luckily very few deck landing accidents.

Our year East of Suez also involved Britain's military involvement in Yemen when communist South Yemen made attempts to take over the British base and strategic port of Aden. Many missions were flown in an area known as the Radfan against the rebels and a number of rebel attacks were made on the port of Aden - in particular in a section called Crater. Once, I had flown to Aden from Nairobi in Kenya, where we had disembarked our aircraft, in order to join HMS Ark Royal, and myself and my navigator (even now known as an Observer in the Royal Navy) had to escape from the Crater area, which we were passing through, due to incessant bombing by the rebels who were demanding independence. Unfortunately, Yemen is now a devastated country with a child dying approximately every ten minutes from the consequences of war - a fact that has been rarely reported in the mainstream media.

After a year East of Suez, we returned to European waters and operated in the North Sea and off northern Scandinavia in NATO operations to intercept and track Soviet Bear and Badger bombers flying down from bases near the city of Archangel. This was at the height of the Cold War and there were many interactions between the Royal and Soviet Navies.

After 175 Gannet deck landings, including 50 at night, I converted to the twin boom all weather Sea Vixen fighter for a further two year carrier tour and another year East of Suez. This was followed by my transition to F4Bs and F4Js with the US Navy, during my time at the Naval Air Station NAS Miramar in California with Top Gun, followed by a further two years flying the F4K back on board HMS Ark Royal with the Royal Navy.

# Chapter 6

## East of Suez Revisited

After my first tour of duty East of Suez flying the Fairey Gannet off the aircraft carrier HMS Ark Royal, I was sent to the north of Scotland to learn fighter tactics on the single seat Hawker Hunter - a swept wing jet fighter that I had previously flown during Advanced Flying Training in Wales. The Air Warfare Instructors (AWI) Course was based at RNAS Lossiemouth - known to all as Lossie - and, with its staff pilots, I learned the rudiments of fighter combat including aerial gunnery and firing two inch rockets and dropping bombs in diving attacks on a number of ranges both on land and at sea.

Lossie was an ideal location to practise fighter combat down to a low level in the mountains since the north of Scotland was scarcely populated and we had free range of the majority of the Highlands in which to practise our manoeuvres. Looking back on it, I'm amazed that there were so few complaints about our antics - and even fewer accidents. These antics often involved a four plane strike flight of Hunters, escorted by two other Hunters, flying at very low level along a tortuous route to attack a simulated target. The escorts' role was to protect the strike flight from the "enemy" - the "enemy" (bogeys) being two further Hunters who were lurking hidden in the hills and glens along the attack route. Inevitably, when the strike flight was intercepted by the "enemy", all hell would break loose and the ensuing engagement would result in four Hunters at perhaps fifty feet above the ground engaging each other in high G slashing attacks as the other four aircraft - the strike flight - endeavoured to reach its intended target.

The AWI Course took first class pilots from their front line squadrons and trained them to a high level before sending them back to their squadrons to instruct the other pilots in fighter combat and air-to-ground manoeuvres. The AWI Course was founded 10 years before the US Navy's Top Gun school was formed at Naval Air Station (NAS) Miramar in San Diego by an Act of Congress as a result of the initial poor fighter combat kill ratios with the North Vietnamese. As a subsequent staff pilot with the first cadre of Top Gun pilots in California, I have always felt that the concept of Top Gun was taken from the program developed by the Royal Navy's AWI Course. Of course, many of my fellow USN pilots still object to this suggestion and we now good naturedly agree to disagree.

Being so far north in Scotland, night flying in the summer required operating further south due to the incessant daylight and, in fact, the town of Lossiemouth always had a golf tournament that teed off at midnight on midsummer's eve - such was the lack of darkness at that time of year. Lossie was, I believe, the first airfield anywhere to introduce falcons to chase away the seagulls that gathered at the end of the runways. These flocks of large birds often caused bird strikes against aircraft - the worst bird strike occurring when a gull was ingested in an engine on take off. If this happened to a single engine jet fighter - such as the Hunter - the result was sometimes a low level pilot ejection. Falcons and hawks are now being used in the USA in order to bring down small privately owned radio controlled drones that are rapidly becoming a menace around airfields and public open air events.

Interestingly, Gordonstoun School, which both Prince Philip and Prince Charles attended, sits off the end of one of Lossie's runways. If that runway was the active take off runway and school was in session, the Control Tower would announce "Up School" when clearing the pilot for take off. This required the pilot to make a sharp turn immediately after lift off to avoid blasting over the top of the school.

Being so far away from the likes of London, or even Edinburgh, entertainment - official and unofficial - was dreamed up on the air station itself. One amusing incident occurred in the Wardroom (Officers Mess) which was an old Nissen or Quonset-style hut from WWII. The bar in the Wardroom had a central coal fireplace and chimney and one evening a visiting US Navy Admiral was being entertained in the bar when a pilot, nicknamed Fred, managed to crawl along in the space above the ceiling to the flue above the fireplace - armed with a foam fire extinguisher. Meanwhile, the congenial and unsuspecting Admiral, in dress uniform with medals down to his waist, had been lured close to the fireplace in time for Fred to deliver his fire extinguisher down the flue with the resulting foam and coal dust engulfing the distinguished guest.

After my time in Scotland, I converted onto the De Havilland Sea Vixen at RNAS Yeovilton in Somerset and joined my front line squadron on HMS Eagle where I served for a further two years flying the Vixen - mostly East of Suez again. Serving on board Eagle meant a lot to me as my father had been Captain of the previous Eagle on the China Station leading up to WWII. His Eagle had originally been commissioned by the Chilean Navy as a battleship to be called the Almirante Cochrane but the British Government bought her while under construction and converted her to an aircraft carrier. She served with distinction throughout the early years of WWII with her days ending when she was sunk by a German U boat in the Mediterranean to the south of Majorca during Operation Pedestal. Luckily for our family, my father had moved on to a shore position at the Admiralty in London by the time of the sinking.

The Sea Vixen was a twin-boom two seat two engine carrier-based all weather jet fighter with the capability of firing two inch rockets, launching Firestreak and Red Top air-to-air missiles, tossing Lepus flares and dropping 250 lb and 500 lb bombs. The odd feature in its design was that the Observer (Navigator) sat entombed in the fuselage to the right of and below the pilot whose hands on the stick were all the Observer could see of the pilot's actions. In front of the Observer were the radar for controlling interceptions, the armament panel, an airspeed indicator (ASI) and the fuel switches. It's amazing that Observers stuck it out in these claustrophobic conditions in what we called the "Coal Hole". Relying on the pilot to get the beast back onboard the carrier at night, without the Observer having any vision ahead, required a very strong nerve. One Observer did decide, just before take off from a runway ashore, that he'd had enough and, opening the hatch above his head, leaped out and ran off into the undergrowth. The hatch was the Observer's only means of entry and exit to his ejection seat but he did have a small window on the right hand side which gave him enough sideways vision to add to the fear level.

Landings on Eagle's angled deck by trapping one of the four arrester wires with the aircraft's tailhook and the thrill of the steam catapult launches off Eagle's bow were very exhilarating. Launches involved the aircraft hurtling down the short steam catapult track from a standing start, being slung into the air and hopefully achieving a flying speed of around 150 mph by the time the Vixen reached the end of the short catapult track. Landing involved three variables - line up on the centreline of the angled deck, accurate airspeed dependent on the aircraft's weight and the correct glide path to catch the ideal number three wire - the third wire from the stern of the ship. Visual glide path information was provided by the green "meatball" on the projector sight that was mounted on the port (left) side of the carrier's deck in full view of the approaching pilot. A high approach and the meatball would ride high, a low approach and the meatball would go low, a very low approach would cause the meatball to turn red and, if very very low, the meatball would start flashing. A very very low approach would result in the aircraft hitting the stern of the carrier - known as the round down.

By the time my two year Vixen tour was over, I had achieved a further 188 deck landings of which 44 were at night. This, added to my earlier Gannet deck landings, brought my combined total of deck landings at that time to 363 with 94 of them at night.

My operational tour of duty East of Suez on Eagle initially involved a stop at Ascension Island in the Atlantic before pulling into Cape Town in South Africa for a few days. This was a sort of homecoming for me having spent some of my childhood about thirty miles south of Cape Town on False Bay in Simon's Town and I met up with old friends of my parents including the ex-Mayor of Cape Town who invited me to a day's horse racing at Cape Town's primary racecourse - Kenilworth. Other friends managed Rhodes Fruit Farms in the Stellenbosch/Paarl area - inland from Cape Town and close to the wonderful old French Huguenot town of Franschhoek where some of the finest South African grapes are grown.

After South Africa, we operated off Gan in the Maldive Islands south of India and along the Malaysian peninsular including off the island of Penang before docking in the Naval Dockyard in Singapore. There, the squadrons of Sea Vixens, Buccaneers and Gannets disembarked to various RAF airfields on Singapore island with my squadron deployed to RAF Changi which is now

Singapore's main international airport. Whereas my fellow pilots lived ashore in RAF barracks, I was fortunate to have a friend who was a colonial officer with the Hong Kong Shanghai Bank (HKSB) in Singapore. In those colonial days, HKSB officers abroad were not allowed to get married until they had completed at least one tour of duty overseas and these pampered gentlemen lived in what was called the Bank Mess.

My friend's old colonial mansion was far from a Mess and the young officers had cooks and servants to provide them with the necessities of life. I was offered a room in this mansion any time I was ashore and I always remember taking a bath upon my first arrival (the colonists had no showers in those days) and finding that all my clothes had been removed after I had completed my ablutions. Sure enough, a Chinese steward had already washed and dried them and was now ironing them in the corridor outside my room.

Golf was a favourite pastime for us pilots when we weren't flying and we had access to such fine golf courses as the Royal Singapore Golf Course and those on Penang and in northern Malaysia - and subsequently in Hong Kong. I also enjoyed the horse racing at Bukit Timah racecourse in Singapore and at Happy Valley on Hong Kong island - horse racing which fueled the insatiable Chinese appetite for gambling. The quality of the thoroughbreds at these two racecourses was surprisingly high.

In addition to our stops in Singapore, we also operated off and docked in Hong Kong and we were often given time off to explore the island and the New Territories, as they were called, on the mainland side of Hong Kong - not far from Kowloon. The Army's Royal Anglian Regiment were based in Stanley on the far side of Hong Kong island and the Colonel of this regiment thought it would be a good idea if a number of our pilots saw what Army life was like - or so he said. In return, some of his officers would spend time on board HMS Eagle. None of us pilots volunteered so I and two others were ordered ashore to fulfill the Colonel's request. Upon arrival at the Stanley barracks, the Colonel greeted us with open arms and told us he knew full well why we had volunteered - to get off that blasted ship for a few days. Rest assured he said, there would be nothing military about our stay with his regiment. Instead, we had free run of the officers' bar, drivers to take us into the capital Victoria and the use of his swimming pool and tennis courts at all times. Needless to say, we had a marvellous stay and learned, when back onboard our carrier, that the Army officers with whom we had exchanged, had been subject to lengthy days in the stinking Engine and Boiler Rooms onboard and had had to spend hours servicing the catapults and other unpleasant and dirty tasks. A section of Victoria is called Wanchai and the umbrella sold there in the street markets was always known as a "Wanchai Burberry" after the name of a well known British raincoat. It became a tradition to always buy one on visits to Hong Kong.

One of my non-flying roles in Eagle was that of Horse Racing Correspondent for the ship's newspaper - the Eagle Express - and my nom de plume was, and still is, Captain Cuttle. Captain Cuttle had won the Epsom Derby in 1922 ridden by the legendary jockey from that time - Steve Donaghue. I've always loved horse racing and that autumn there was an excellent Irish two year old called Sir Ivor which I told the entire ship's company to back at all costs for next June's Epsom Derby.

At the time, I was also a member of the ship's squash team and in Hong Kong we played a number of matches at the Hong Kong Cricket Club where the opposing teams were organised by a puisne judge - Sir Ivo Rigby. It was just too much of a coincidence and Sir Ivor duly won the Epsom Derby and I was feted by all and sundry onboard for my tip in the ship's newspaper.

However, earlier in the same year, while at sea without any radio news contact, I had pretended, on the day of the race, to be the official commentator for the important steeplechase - the Grand National. Needless to say, my "winner" - Dagmar Gittell - did not distinguish itself in the real Grand National and my pretence was soon rumbled.

My Observer at that time on Vixens was a South African with an eye for a gamble and he and I ran a book in the Wardroom as to where Eagle would spend Christmas that year. Hot favourite was Singapore with Hong Kong a close second but we suckered the punters into placing bets at long odds on such as Perth in Western Australia, the Cocos Islands, Christmas Island, Penang and other unlikely venues. Needless to say, we spent Christmas in Singapore but my South African mate and I still made a profit.

The times we spent ashore made up for the long days and nights at sea flying our aircraft in all conditions - often with no diversionary airfields and with a Buccaneer tanker sitting overhead the carrier - especially at night - in the event that too many futile attempts to get back aboard resulted in a lack of fuel.

One fun deployment was to the Royal Australian Air Force base (RAAF) at Pearce in Western Australia - not far from Perth. Not only was the low flying in the Outback quite sensational but all my Moody cousins live on the Swan River near Perth and one cousin, another Richard Moody, lent me a car for the duration which meant that I was able to visit Aboriginal towns, such as Manjimup, and explore the delightful area in the southwest corner of Western Australia called Margaret River where some fine white wines are produced.

Eagle also operated with the US Navy off the Philippines and we disembarked our aircraft to the Naval Air Station at Cubi Point while Eagle docked in Subic Bay. It was in the Officers Mess at Cubi Point that I learned how to lose at liar's dice - a game I've never played since.

Our time in the Far East and in the Antipodes came to an end and we headed back across the Indian Ocean operating off Muscat and Oman, the island of Salalah and the strategic port of Aden which is very much in today's news with the destruction of Yemen by Saudi Arabia – sadly with the complicity of the USA and other countries including the UK. It was then up the Red Sea, through the Suez Canal and back to home port in Plymouth in southwest England via a stop in Gibraltar along the way.

Our flying operations were not over and, after a short period of rest and recreation (R & R), Eagle headed to Iceland and then to the top of Norway to intercept the Soviet Bison and Badger bombers that were coming down from northern Russia in displays of strength and intimidation. I, and many other Vixen pilots, hooked up with the Russians - always in a peaceful fashion - and no unpleasant incidents took place. In fact, on one interception, my Vixen had a photographic pod on one wing and I flew up and down the side of a Badger at a distance of no more than 50 feet snapping pictures of this large bomber and I have a lovely framed picture of a close up shot of the Badger with white fluffy clouds in the background. There was no animosity among the opposing pilots and one of our crews displayed a Playboy centerfold from his cockpit to the Russian bomber crew - much to their delight - and one US Navy aircraft flew alongside a Russian bomber after its ordnance crew had mounted the aircraft's Sidewinder missiles facing backwards as a spoof. Needless to say the Russians got very excited that NATO now had a backwards firing missile which, of course, was not true.

After a stimulating two years of fun and games plus the exhilaration of carrier operations punctuated with moments of sheer terror, my Sea Vixen days came to an end. Sheer terror when facing a heaving and corkscrewing flight deck in the middle of the night when low on fuel and with no diversionary airfield within hundreds of miles. But I survived and prepared to join the US Navy at NAS Miramar in California for another exciting period in my life as an aviator.

# Chapter 7

## TOPGUN, Yuma Arizona and the Mediterranean

I flew to San Diego to take up my duties with the United States Navy at Naval Air Station (NAS) Miramar in California and was greeted at the airport by a fellow fighter pilot who drove me to the bachelor snake ranch which would be my accommodation, with three other pilots from my new F 4 squadron - VF 121 - for the next few years.

The name of the ranch was a rather crude variation of the word Ponderosa which I cannot reveal in polite company. Suffice it to say that, coming from dank and dreary Great Britain, the kidney shaped swimming pool, the palm trees with coloured lights and an extensive sound system and the sliding glass doors which led out onto an expansive patio and down to the swimming pool made me realise that I'd probably hit the jackpot.

The first of my new room mates soon drove up in his white Austin Healey sports car and entered the house wearing shorts, drinking a milkshake and reading Eldridge Cleaver's "Soul on Ice". Needless to say, Flan, as we called him, was no longer a naval officer but a student majoring in Political Science at the University of California in San Diego. I soon learned that he had come to his senses about the militarism we had all been brainwashed into believing in and was now studying the other side of the argument. His Austin Healey prompted me to buy a British racing green MGB GT to remind me of my connections with dear old Blighty and the Royal Navy that I'd left behind.

My first requirement at Miramar was to obtain my Instrument Rating flying the two seat Skyhawk TA4F and I then converted onto the Phantom F4B and F4J with VF 121 - the squadron known as the RAG - or Replacement Air Group - where all future carrier based F4 pilots were trained in the art of interceptions, air combat manoeuvering (ACM) and ground attack.

I was then appointed as the squadron Ordnance Officer in charge of a large team of enlisted sailors who assisted me with all the ordnance that the F4 carried when firing missiles and rockets and dropping bombs. This weaponry included Sidewinder and Sparrow missiles, 2.75 inch rockets, 5 inch Zuni rockets, the Mark 4 Gun Pod, 250 lb and 500 lb bombs and Napalm and there appeared to be no limit regarding the amount of ordnance we could drop on the many ranges in the desert to the east of San Diego.

My role as Squadron Ordnance Officer required me to lead flights of pilots once a month to Marine Corps Air Station (MCAS) Yuma in Arizona for an intensive 10 days of Air to Ground weaponry on the various ranges whose interesting call sign names were such as Rakish Litter and Kitty Baggage. Another Air to Air range on Santa Catalina Island off the coast of California had the amusing call sign of Ruthless Ruth.

My own flights of four F4s, which I led at Yuma, were known as Moody's Blues and flying commenced as early as 5 am due to the intense heat in the desert. I remember one late night out in town when the temperature at midnight on Yuma's main street was 100F. Because of the heat, flying would end soon after midday when all of us would repair to the Officers Club's swimming pool with cocktails in hand. The Officers Club was not far from Yuma's runway and sometimes an F4 was required to be delivered to Yuma from Miramar. A contest developed where the delivering pilot attempted to break the subsonic speed record from Miramar to Yuma and was then required to fly at 400 knots over the runway before breaking down wind pulling as many Gs as possible so his aircraft would fly between the swimming pool and Yuma's runway. I managed to hold the record for this childish game until a pilot named Mugs not only broke closer to the swimming pool than I had but also lowered his landing gear and flew upside down between the pool and runway.

Another amusing incident was when I was asked to drive to Yuma from Miramar in advance of a forthcoming detachment - along with callsign Gator who owned a motorbike. This was in the days that Interstate 8 was still being built from San Diego to Yuma and, in the darkness, it appeared to us that the highway had been completed. It wasn't until my mate on his bike, up ahead, was having to gun his throttle and then, looking down, saw a long groove in the wet concrete behind him that we realised that all was not well. Sure enough, up ahead of us were the lights of the concrete laying equipment whose driver had luckily not spotted our stupidity. I was sufficiently far behind in my MGB to be driving on reasonably solid concrete and we were both able to sneak off into the desert without being detected.

Fortunately for me, I was in the right place at the right time when the Navy Fighter Weapons School - TOPGUN - was formed and the new school's Skipper (Commanding Officer) - callsign Yank - asked me to join his team of instructors and he sent me to MCAS El Toro south of Los Angeles to qualify on the single seat A4E Skyhawk. The concept of TOPGUN was to take top quality pilots from their carrier squadrons and train them to the highest level of air combat manoeuvring. The initial kill ratios in the early days of the war in Vietnam against the North Vietnamese pilots, flying their MIG 17s and 21s, were poor and TOPGUN was designed to greatly improve the success rate by training selected front line pilots who then went back to their squadrons to train other pilots to a higher level of fighter combat. The formation of TOPGUN was the result of a study - carried out by Captain Frank Ault - known as the "Ault Report".

In ACM training, it's important to "fight" against aircraft with dissimilar performances to those of one's own and the A4E - known as the Mongoose - was the ideal aircraft to train against since its performance was very similar to that of the MIGs. In addition to this, the F4 did not perform well fighting in the horizontal, such as the MIGs did, and so a method of fighting in the vertical - known as Energy Maneuverability - was developed where the power of the F4's two General Electric engines would easily allow the F4 pilot to get above his opponent and perform slashing downward attacks before screaming skywards again. The Mongoose was even painted in MIG colours and I flew many hours as the "Aggressor" pilot helping to improve the level of fighter combat in the F4 world.

Every fighter pilot has a call sign and all my fellow US Navy TOPGUN pilots used macho call signs such as Rattler, Viper, Condor, Cougar, Hawkeye, Gator, Yank etc but I decided to downplay the machismo and chose the very

English Cholmondeley (pronounced Chumley) and to this day I'm still known as Cholmondeley by many of my flying friends. Cholmondeley is an ancient Norman last name that first appeared in the Domesday Book in 1086.

Apart from the constant dogfighting, missile firing and air to ground dive bombing that we carried out, we also had the task of delivering F4s to the Vietnam theater. I did not have US citizenship in those days so, thankfully, I was never sent to WestPac, as it was called, to carry out the destruction of Vietnam, Laos and Cambodia. But I did deliver an F4 to Naval Air Station Atsugi in Japan for onward delivery to the combat zone. Known as a TransPac, an abbreviation for Trans Pacific, myself and my back seat RIO (Radar Intercept Officer) departed Miramar and refuelled from a slow flying propeller driven KC 130 tanker before landing at Honolulu for the night. Then it was on to Wake Island the next day - again refuelling along the way from a KC 130 - before arriving at Atsugi on the third day after further in-flight refueling. Aerial refueling in a high performance F4 from a slow flying KC 130 tanker was an interesting exercise which involved plugging into the tanker's streamed basket at high altitude at an uncomfortably slow speed for the F4. To alleviate the slow speed discomfort, once the F4 was plugged in, the tanker would start downhill picking up speed to make for a more comfortable ride for the F4. This was known as "Tobogganing". Once topped up, the F4 would unplug and zoom back up to cruising altitude and arrive at the designated destination some hours before the tanker plodded in.

One of my fellow aviators in TOPGUN was Goose whose call sign, along with Viper and Cougar, was one of only three original call signs used in the now famous movie. The real Goose was from Rhinelander Wisconsin and, as an RIO he subsequently flew in my back seat for a year in the Royal Navy aboard the carrier HMS Ark Royal. Goose was the first aviator to successfully eject four times (once in Viet Nam) using the British built Martin Baker ejection seat and he was invited to a dinner in his honour in London by Sir James Martin - Chairman of Martin Baker. Sadly, Goose was subsequently killed in a mid-air collision in an F14 fighter off Puerto Rico.

I too ejected, but only once, when my F4 caught fire over the Pacific to the west of La Jolla California. Some would say that I set fire to myself as the flames from my afterburner, during a fighter tactics mission, set fire to fuel which, unbeknownst to me, was leaking from the fuel cells in the back of my aircraft. My fire was the first of a number of similar accidents and it took some time for anyone to realise what was causing these fires. My ejection, at around 10,000 feet, was smooth and successful. Although the firing of my ejection seat subjected me to 22G vertically (22 times the force of gravity), I had managed to slow the beast down to around 220 knots (250 mph) and all systems worked and I was eventually picked up from my life raft by a Coast Guard helicopter after spending 10 minutes in my parachute before splashing into the Pacific Ocean. Amazingly I took, and passed, my already planned annual physical the next day without the surgeon knowing about my ejection.

The call sign Viper was used by a white haired fellow pilot who was given a small part in the movie TOPGUN - having been appointed the Technical Adviser for the production. As he told me, all through the making of the movie, Viper kept telling the English Director, Tony Scott, that this was not the way we did it in TOPGUN. To which Tony replied that he wasn't at all concerned about the true TOPGUN - all he wanted to do was attract as many movie goers as possible to enjoy his production - a production which turned out to be one of the best selling movies of all time.

Rumour has it that Viper was made two offers as remuneration for his technical advice - one a considerable lump sum, the other a small percentage of the box office revenue for life. Believing it to be a poor movie, he took the lump sum but realised he'd made a serious mistake when he went to the movie for the first time and saw how much the audience was captivated by the excitement of the flying and Tom Cruise's performance. Sadly, Tony Scott committed suicide some years ago by jumping off the San Pedro bridge in southern California.

Amazingly, in those far off days, we were able to fly an F4 anywhere in the Continental USA over a weekend and I flew to Boston and Chicago and often flew to Florida with one of my roommates who was now engaged to a girl who had graduated from Butler University in Indianapolis. Eventually, the day of their nuptials arrived and I flew to Key West in Florida in an F4 for the wedding, put on my white officer's uniform and was a sword carrying member of the honour guard. There in the wedding party was the bride's roommate from Butler who had flown in from Germany where she was teaching. Needless to say, I fell head over heels in love and proposed marriage after 72 hours in each other's presence and, over 50 years later, husband and wife are still speaking to each other.

I guess Lisa didn't stand a chance of resisting a uniformed fighter pilot who had flown his F4 from California to be an usher at this glamorous wedding held at Vizcaya, the estate built by James Deering of International Harvester fame, close to Key Biscayne. To announce our engagement, we held a subsequent surprise party back at the Ponderosa in San Diego where four gate-crashing fellow pilots gave us a "moonshot" - in celebration of the recently successful Apollo 11 moon landing - with the letters and numbers - AP - OL - LO - 11 - painted on the appropriate parts of their anatomy.

The snake ranch, where I had lived until getting married, was very much party central since, for some extraordinary reason, I was able to order unlimited duty free wine and spirits through the British Embassy in Washington DC and our orders were flown across country to us once a month so we were able to hold regular lengthy weekend parties which always seemed to end with everybody in the swimming pool in the wee hours of the morning. The beverage of choice was a nasty concoction which we called a Fish Wife's Breath - real name Fish House Punch - which had been introduced to me on the Royal Yacht - but not by Her Majesty.

Shortly after our hurriedly arranged wedding back in England, Lisa and I were invited to a cocktail party onboard a Royal Navy frigate which was visiting San Diego. After the party, the Captain, a South African friend of mine and a fellow naval pilot, invited the two of us to join him and two of his officers at dinner in a local restaurant on the water called the Chart House. Lisa was dressed in a white suit with a gold body chain and the rest of us were wearing white tuxedos. After giving the restaurant's hostess our last name - Moody - we were told that there would be a one hour wait for a table. At which time, Lisa announced that we were the British rock group, the Moody Blues. We were immediately ushered to a table overlooking the Pacific Ocean where a member of the wait staff took our orders and then returned with a Moody Blues' LP record and asked us all to sign it - which we did. My South African friend then turned to Lisa and told her that she was on her own if the restaurant asked us to sing a number - such as the appropriate Moody Blues hit - "Nights in White Satin".

It was then time to re-join the Royal Navy and Goose and I were appointed to the RN's only Phantom squadron - onboard HMS Ark Royal. I was made the Senior Pilot of the squadron which flew the F4K - similar to the F4J but with Rolls Royce Speys instead of J79 General Electric engines. By this time, the

British Empire was slowly crumbling so it was no more East of Suez operations. Instead, with the Cold War in full cry, the majority of our operations were in the Mediterranean, often operating from Decimomannu on Sardinia, plus in NATO shows of strength off northern Scandinavia with time also spent with the US Navy (USN) off the east coast of the USA, including Key West, and down in the Caribbean off Puerto Rico. Ports of call included Fort Lauderdale, Jacksonville, New York, Gibraltar, Malta, Athens and Bergen and Oslo in Norway - all nice cities but not quite as exotic as those Far Eastern havens of days gone by. A lot of time was spent "cross decking" where I would take a flight of four F4Ks onboard a much larger USN carrier for two weeks of NATO operations. We also spent time flying with the German Navy's F 104s out of Schleswig in Schleswig-Holstein and operating with the French Navy's Air Arm - the Aeronavale - out of Landivisiau in Brittany which was flying the F8 Crusader.

During my time operating the F4K off HMS Ark Royal, I carried out a further 214 day deck landings and 50 at night. This gave me final figures of 483 day deck landings and 144 at night for a total of 627 deck landings in all - flying the Gannet, Sea Vixen and Phantom off various aircraft carriers. And I lived to tell the tale.

But the British Labor government had by now decided to scrap all future aircraft carrier construction and so I decided to move on. I tendered my resignation from the Royal Navy but Their Lordships at the Admiralty, in their wisdom, would not let me leave the RN for another 2 years so I spent an idyllic time flying VIPs in two communications aircraft - the De Havilland Sea Devon (DH 104) and the De Havilland Sea Heron (DH 114) - the first piston aircraft I had ever flown. And the RN was kind enough to allow me, and others, to obtain our ATPLs (Airline Transport Pilot's Licences) using these piston aircraft and this kind gesture served me well in obtaining subsequent employment with BOAC (British Overseas Airways Corporation). My qualification on the DH 114 also held me in good stead when I went to fly for St Lucia Airways in the Caribbean after being put on fully paid "furlough" by BOAC which by then had become British Airways.

899 Squadron Crest - Sea Viven - Royal Navy

Phantom F4K landing on HMS Ark Royal - Royal Navy

Soviet Badger bomber off northern Norway

Hunter GA 11 - Royal Navy

A4E "Mongoose" TOPGUN - US Navy

The Author with the real "Goose" - US Navy

# Chapter 8

## British Overseas Airways Corporation/British Airways – BOAC/BA

---

Upon leaving the Royal Navy, my South African navigator friend talked me into arranging an interview with Ross Perot's company - du Pont Flore Gorgan - an investment broking house in New York City. At the same time, I heard that British Overseas Airways Corporation (BOAC) was hiring pilots and, as I had already obtained my Airline Transport Pilot's Licence (ATPL), I decided instead to go for an interview to be a commercial long haul airline pilot. I reasoned that if I did not like airline flying I could always try my luck as a stockbroker but the opposite would probably not be possible.

Having fumbled my way through the interview with a very proper gentleman wearing a tailcoat and pinstripe trousers and being offered a job, I showed up at the BOAC headquarters at London's Heathrow Airport with eleven other potential airline pilots - nine of whom being ex Royal Air Force (RAF) and only two of us being ex Royal Navy (RN).

We were promptly told that our ground school and flying training on the Vickers VC 10 would be delayed for four months and that we would be on full non-flying pay until a course became available. So I spent the next few months working in a fish and chip shop owned by an Italian - Umberto Valdembrini - who had recently been laid off from an executive role with Newsweek in London.

Eventually, we were called back by BOAC, passed our ground school exams, spent hours in the flight simulator and then commenced a brief session of flying training on the VC10. Luckily, our training Captain appeared to prefer golf to flying and so we positioned our VC10 at Prestwick airport on the west coast of Scotland in order to be close to a number of fine golf courses - such as Turnberry, Western Gailes, Old Prestwick and Troon. Needless to say, we did indeed play many rounds of golf on these historic courses (and some real tennis in Troon) as well as being checked out for our role as a Co-Pilot on international services around the world. The majority of our flying was practising touch and gos at Shannon Airport in Ireland.

The VC 10 - Standard, Super and Superb models - was nimble for an airliner and had a capacity of up to 175 passengers with a flight deck crew of three - Captain, Co-Pilot and Flight Engineer - and a maximum of six stewards and/or stewardesses. It was very stable on the approach and easy to land and had massive appeal with the flying public. Unfortunately, it came at a time when the Boeing 707 was in extensive production and many more 707s were sold around the world than the attractive VC10 which was only operated by a few African and Middle Eastern airlines in addition to BOAC.

BOAC covered the majority of the world with the exception of West Africa, South America and Europe - the latter being covered by British European Airways (BEA). Our network was mind boggling in its variety and cosmopolitan nature and I was fortunate to fly throughout the Middle East, East Africa, the Indian subcontinent, Asia (including Hong Kong and Japan), North America, Australia and New Zealand. In fact, my very first service was operating to Beirut in Lebanon and on to Tehran in Iran - two cities very much in the news these days.

Airline flying in those days was a far cry from the current horrors of commercial aviation and the Transportation Security System (TSA) and, although the odd hi-jacking did take place, passengers were welcome to come up to the flight deck whose door was always open. Passengers dressed up in the nicest clothes, were very polite to the cabin and flight deck crews and were always very appreciative of the service which we provided.

Airline flying, after throwing fighters onto the heaving flight deck of a twisting aircraft carrier, was 95% boredom and 5% excitement and the VC 10 had an efficient autopilot that could be slaved to the Inertial Navigation System (INS) which, although not as accurate as today's GPS or SatNav, could still get the aircraft to within about two miles of its destination. Conventional methods of landing the aircraft were then used - such as Radar and the Instrument Landing System (ILS).

The moments of utter boredom were sometimes interrupted by exciting events such as the day we ran off the end of the runway in a monsoon in Rangoon in Burma - known today as Yangon in Myanmar. The monsoon had just arrived in the area and the airport control tower had assured us that braking action on the runway was good - a fact we soon discovered to be blatantly untrue when the aircraft's anti-lock braking system (ABS) showed us that the surface of the runway was a skating rink. The ABS forced us to roll out over a far greater length of runway than normal in order to avoid bursting tires. Unfortunately, our roll-out was longer than the runway itself and we ended up in the mud close to a ravine beyond the end of the paved surface. Everybody onboard was unharmed and transportation soon showed up and took the passengers to the terminal.

In order to protect our interests in any subsequent investigation, we decided to visit the control tower to obtain recordings of the radio interchanges between us and the air traffic controllers. It was quite a shock to enter the control tower and meet the bare chested air traffic controllers who were wearing nothing but "longyi" - Burmese skirts. The crew and passengers had been interned in a hotel in Rangoon while an investigation was carried out since our clearance had only been to transit Burma (a closed country at that time) on our way to Singapore and Darwin. Fortunately, we were cleared of any pilot error after a few days and the frustrated passengers re-embarked and we flew on to their final destinations.

Another incident, which came to mind after reading about the treatment meted out not long ago by United Airlines to a Vietnamese doctor who wouldn't give up his seat, became known in the family as the "Cairo Affair". Cairo always was a hell-hole of an airport with every passenger desperate to get out of the then sweaty non air conditioned terminal and onto a cooler airliner.

In this incident, all the passengers had boarded our full aircraft when an Egyptian catering truck driver drove his vehicle into the open front door of our aircraft. Unfortunately, the escape slide, which was hanging on the door, was damaged beyond repair which meant that eight of the seats onboard around this door could not be occupied for takeoff or landing and the flight was full. Seven benign first class passengers did leave the aircraft at our request but the eighth - a Texas oil man - flatly refused to do so saying he was flying to London to sign the most important deal of his life. Not only did he scream and yell but he took our names and said he'd write a serious letter of complaint to the Chairman of British Airways (BA) as BOAC had now become.

We decided to have a council of war on the flight deck and chose one of our lovely stewardesses to serve the irate passenger with copious amounts of champagne until it was time for take off - at which time we'd invite the Texan up onto the flight deck to witness the take off from the jump seat before going back to his seat. This we did and his demeanour soon mellowed and he was as good as gold for the rest of the four hour flight. Luckily, the arrival into London Heathrow was from the east over the Thames, the Tower of London, Tower Bridge and the Houses of Parliament so again we invited him onto the flight deck for a landing of a lifetime.

He did indeed write a letter to the Chairman of BA but not the detrimental one he had threatened us with. Instead, we were all forwarded an amazing letter of commendation which he'd sent to the Chairman in which he had stated that we were the finest crew he'd ever experienced. It's hard to say what we would have done in this situation with today's paranoid post 9/11 procedures which involve the flight deck door being locked at all times.

To illustrate how different airline flying was in those days, my eight year old daughter flew with me on the jump seat from London to Cairo and on to Khartoum in Sudan and back and was even encouraged to serve the passengers in First Class. I took her in a taxi from Khartoum to the confluence of the Blue and White Niles in Omdurman where she hid below the taxi's rear seats as the locals crowded around the vehicle to get their first glimpse of a little blonde European girl. Lisa, also accompanied me on one trip for two weeks, again on the jump seat, when I flew a commercial service from Johannesburg to the Seychelles and on to Malawi and Dar-es-Salaam in Tanzania and then up to Cyprus before returning to London.

Other excitements were experiencing an engine failure on take off out of London Heathrow and an attempted interception by Libyan fighter jets off the coast of Libya. The latter incident occurred when a strike of Greek air traffic controllers caused our flight from London to Cairo to be re-routed over Tripoli in Libya before turning eastwards and proceeding to Egypt. At that time, relations between Libya and Egypt were not good and, for some strange reason, the Libyan air traffic controllers were convinced that we, in our innocent VC 10, were an Egyptian bomber and they ordered us to land in

Tripoli. Ignoring this order, we thrust the throttles to full bore and screamed out of Libyan airspace and into Egyptian airspace, shaking off any Libyan fighters, and scrambled into Cairo.

One hijacking near miss occurred in Dubai after we had handed over the aircraft to another crew in Kuwait. This new crew flew the service to nearby Dubai where the VC 10 was attacked by gunmen who, disguised as aircraft maintenance workers in white overalls, burst out of the terminal and machine gunned the plane and injured the Indian stewardess who was standing by the opened rear passenger door. The aircraft was then seized by the gunmen who ordered the Captain to fly the plane to Tunis before finally giving themselves up after shooting a German passenger and dumping him on the tarmac.

An amusing incident occurred when another VC 10 crew, staying the night in a hotel in Moscow, gathered in a hotel room on the first floor up for cocktails as they were not required to fly for another forty eight hours. One crew member surmised that the room was probably bugged. At which time another crew member pulled up the carpet in the center of the room to discover a small bolt. Thinking that this might be a bug, he unscrewed it to see what it was. Shortly thereafter, there was a frantic knocking on the hotel room door and a member of the hotel staff burst in screaming in Russian that the chandelier in the ceiling in the main lobby had crashed to the floor.

The overnight stopovers in our far away destinations were very long by today's standards and BA was kind enough to provide sail boats and make arrangements for us to play golf at top notch courses in such as Calcutta, New Delhi and at the old colonial Hill Club in Nuwara Eliya in the mountains not far from Kandy on what is now the island of Sri Lanka but was then Ceylon. Playing golf on the Indian subcontinent was less of a sport and more like entertainment. A four ball would involve a team of twelve traipsing around an idyllic golf course since each of the four golfers would not only have one caddie each but also an "agie wallah" - an "ahead or fore caddy". The secret to choosing one's agie wallah was to select one with splayed toes as, without shoes, those with the largest gap between their toes were better capable of picking the ball up with their bare feet and sneaking the ball out onto the fairway when in fact one's drive had disappeared into the rough. Either the agie wallahs were betting on their clients to win the round or they were looking for a large tip.

Only on an Indian golf course would you find two people handling one shovel. One to do the digging and the other to do the lifting - using a rope tied to the bottom of the shaft. And where else would you find five men operating one push mower? One gentleman doing the steering and the other four pushing on two wooden poles lashed horizontally to a rope attached to the front of the mower.

Another fascinating gentleman was the guy in a dhoti sitting shivering on the bank of one of the many ponds (or tanks as they were called) which dotted many of the Indian golf courses. His job was to jot down the name of a golfer and the details of his ball in his notebook should the golfer top his shot into the water. Dhoti-man's job was to wait until there were ten names in his book and then, having dived into the water to retrieve the balls, return the balls to the Clubhouse where golfers could collect their missing balls at the end of their round. However, few golf balls ended up back at the Clubhouse as another gentleman would appear out of the trees at a subsequent hole offering to sell golf balls - one of which being one's own missing ball.

Riding in a taxi in Calcutta was always an exciting experience as all drivers drove on the left hand side, the right hand side and in the middle of the road - when they weren't avoiding the cows, which are sacred, that often wandered down busy streets. On one taxi ride, after asking the driver to let me out, he stopped in the middle of the road. On jumping out, I saw another taxi bearing down on me so I slammed the door shut and leapt out of the way. Unfortunately, the door bounced back open and the oncoming taxi struck it at right angles and drove off with my door firmly positioned on the front of his cab. My driver merely looked at me and shrugged his shoulders as if to say "such is life".

Another fun escapade, in addition to the excitement of arriving at such as Chicago O'Hare in the rush hour after the boredom of a transatlantic crossing, was spending two days on an ancient ferry - built in Glasgow in the 1920s - on a tributary of the Ganges River in Bangladesh which was akin to going back four hundred years in time. There were many brick kilns up the river and square sail flat bottomed boats were used to bring the bricks downstream to Dacca - the capital of Bangladesh. Getting these empty boats back - up river and up wind - to the kilns involved perhaps one hundred men on the river bank hauling on a long rope attached to the top of the mast of each vessel since these ancient barges had no other means of propulsion.

Islamabad, the capital of Pakistan, was another of our destinations and hiking trips were taken to high altitudes in the Hindu Kush and in the Valley of Swat. On one occasion, myself and another crew member flew to Peshawar and then hired a taxi and a Pashtun guide to get us to the Khyber Pass. There, in the border village of Landi Kotal, we fired bullets into the air from small pistols manufactured to look like ballpoint pens and then headed over to the village of Darra Adam Khel where the locals would sit cross legged manufacturing exact working imitations of the assault weapons of that day.

Subsequently, a number of us pilots were offered fully paid "furlough" to stand down from flying with BA. We were to be given three months notice of recall and were required to have a six monthly simulator check in London but the stand down did allow us to fly with any other airline which did not compete with BA. Having contacts on the island of St Lucia in the Caribbean, who told me that St Lucia Airways were looking to hire a pilot with the De Havilland 114 on his licence (which I did have), I had no hesitation in accepting the BA offer and my wife and two kids headed to the Caribbean for another chapter in our lives.

# Chapter 9

## St. Lucia Airways - Life on a Caribbean Island

The island of St Lucia sits at the northern end of the Windward Islands between the islands of Martinique and St Vincent. The Windward Islands being the group of islands, which include Barbados, Trinidad and Tobago, that lie to the south of the Leeward Islands.

The capital of St Lucia, Castries, is on the north end of an island which is dominated by the two mountainous peaks - Gros and Petit Piton ("Big and Small Spike"). These icons lie close to the volcanic region and a town named Soufriere ("Sulphur in the Air" in English) and the lovely beach community of Anse Chastanet - Anse being a French word for "Cove".

Shortly after British Airways (BA) had offered a number of us VC 10 pilots fully paid furlough, as mentioned in the last chapter, I learned that St Lucia Airways were looking for a pilot who was type rated on the De Havilland Heron (DH 114). Fortunately for me, I had flown the Heron during my last few months in the Royal Navy and during this 10 month period had obtained my British Air Transport Pilot's Licence (ATPL). I had also passed my type rating on the Heron and flown VIPs around the British Isles and Europe piloting a Heron for a Naval communications squadron.

I also learned that friends of mine, Nick, originally from Rhodesia (now Zimbabwe) and Pat, originally from South West Africa (now Namibia), had bought Hurricane Hole Hotel on idyllic Marigot Bay on the west side of St Lucia. This is the bay which the author James Michener once described as being the most beautiful bay in all of the Caribbean. It was also the bay where some of the movie "Doctor Doolittle" was shot.

Nick had flown the Supermarine Scimitar on board HMS Ark Royal when I was flying Fairey Gannets and Pat had subsequently been his chef on his large yacht, Cariad, which Nick had bought to operate in the yacht chartering business after he left the Royal Navy. They had sailed Cariad for charter in the Mediterranean and then worked their way across the Atlantic – initially operating out of the island of Grenada before ending up on St Lucia.

Unfortunately for Nick and Pat, but fortunately for me and my family, Hurricane Hole Hotel had been heavily damaged by Hurricane Allen and Nick and Pat needed somebody to caretake their hotel while repairs were being carried out since they owned and operated a successful restaurant on Rodney Bay at the north end of the island.

Lisa jumped at the idea of life on a Caribbean Island, obtained our two young daughters' school curriculums for the next year and encouraged me to agree to the role which I had now been offered by St Lucia Airways. I readily accepted the offer as there would be very little downside to flying in the Caribbean since BA was going to continue to pay me although I was technically on three months notice of recall and would be required to present myself at London Heathrow airport every six months for a flight simulator check.

Life at Hurricane Hole Hotel was nothing if not interesting. We lived in the only barely habitable bungalow where mushrooms grew overnight in the carpet and cockroaches roamed and cooking was initially carried out on a wood fired barbecue since there was no electricity. Lisa, a qualified teacher, taught the girls each morning by the swimming pool after I had removed the very large crabs from the bottom of the pool and the girls were then given the afternoon off to go sailing or water skiing - or even come flying with me. These large crabs spent each night in the pool and were very persistent as they were always at the bottom of the pool the next morning. However, we never did have grilled crab on our barbecue. The hotel did have a wonderful boat boy from Grenada named Julian who taught me to windsurf and would take us all water skiing at the drop of a hat.

Eventually, we were able to remove the diesel generator from Cariad which was docked next to the hotel and this allowed us to supply the hotel with our own electricity but the mushrooms never did go away - nor did the crabs. We also had a small red van for getting around the island and this came in very handy when the diesel tank for the generator needed to be topped up.

The Heron was an ancient four engine piston monoplane with fixed landing gear which carried twenty passengers. St Lucia Airways had purchased three of these aircraft from British European Airways (BEA) but only two had managed to find their way across the Atlantic to St Lucia from the UK. Of these two, only one was in flying condition with the other aircraft sitting in the grass alongside the airport being robbed for spares since parts were in short supply around the world as the Heron was no longer in production. There were two other airlines that I was aware of operating the Heron - albeit with uprated engines - Aspen Airways in Colorado and Prinair (Puerto Rico International Airways).

I first had to obtain my Windward Islands Air Transport Licence and this involved cadging a ride in a local's Cessna 172 to Antigua to present myself to the head aviation civil servant who issued these licences for both the Leeward and the Windward Islands. After hanging around for most of the day, I eventually escaped from his office with licence in hand and, not long after, I learned that this gentleman had previously been head of the Accident Investigation Board but had crashed his plane at the site of an accident that he'd been sent to investigate and had been promptly promoted to the position of head honcho.

I was the only Heron pilot with St Lucia Airways but there were three other pilots - from Belgium, Holland and Germany - who flew the airline's two Britten Norman two engine Islanders and the one three engine Trislander. These smaller aircraft were able to land on tiny islands - such as Union in the Grenadines - whose runways were too short for my lumbering beast. I did have a Canadian maintenance ground engineer but, as he had a keen interest in rum, I kept him as far away as possible from my 30 year old aircraft and I worked on the theory that, if my Heron was in good shape when it landed, it should be perfectly airworthy the next day. As the saying goes in aviation circles - "Kick the Tires and Light the Fires" - and then get airborne.

The Heron did have a co-pilot's seat but, as it could not be sold to fare paying passengers, it was always available for joy rides for Lisa, daughters and friends and many times they took advantage of this as we island hopped around the Caribbean with commercial passengers. The airline was based out of the small airport of Vigie (meaning "Look Out or Crow's Nest") in the north of St Lucia whose runway was too short for most commercial jets which operated out of the much larger airport of Hewanorra, with its longer runway, at the southern end of the island. Hewanorra was the original Carib name for St Lucia and means "Land of the Iguana" in Amerindian.

My destinations were mostly the airports of Grantley Adams on Barbados, Arnos Vale on St Vincent, Fort-de-France on Martinique, Pointe a Pitre on Guadeloupe and Melville Hall on Dominica - the latter being one of the most delightful islands in the Caribbean. Volcanic black sand beaches, 365 waterfalls (one for each day of the year) and still the home of the Caribs in the north of the island from whom the name Caribbean is taken. Being an ardent francophile, Martinique was also a favorite of mine with its excellent food and wine and, not the least, the interesting choice of beachwear - or lack thereof - on its beautiful beaches.

One intriguing contract awarded to St Lucia Airways was for us to supply breadfruit from St Vincent, where it was grown, to the British Airways jumbo which had arrived at Hewanorra airport. Once topped up with breadfruit, the jumbo would then fly its cargo (and passengers) to London for the many West Indians who love breadfruit. To maximise our breadfruit load, my local St Lucian cohort, Danny Fortune, and I would remove all the seats from our aircraft, fly it to St Vincent, stuff the aircraft with boxes of this rather tasteless fruit and then stagger airborne after I had done a swift Load and Balance check to make sure that all would be well.

Unfortunately, we were not able to take off into wind, as is normally done, since the upwind end of the runway at Arnos Vale airport was dominated by a large mountain which we had no chance of clearing with our heavy load. Instead, we did a high speed taxi to the upwind end of the runway, swung the aircraft around, sped off downwind (which was also downhill), lifted the staggering Heron over the sea wall at the end of the runway, kept the aircraft low over the ocean until enough speed was reached so we were then able to climb back over the mountain and head on over to St Lucia. Little did the BA crew waiting at Hewanorra know that I was indeed an employee of their airline since I always wore black pants and a white shirt with a Qantas Captain's four stripe epaulettes which I'd scrounged from an Australian pilot who was moonlighting in the Caribbean.

The only other bit of excitement, apart from landing on runways which were short and often out of sight until turning onto final approach, was the day I was unable to start one of the engines after picking up some German yachtsmen on St Vincent and flying them up to Hewanorra. I was now on my own with the need to get the aircraft back to Vigie and I worked on the theory that there was nothing wrong with the misbehaving engine - it was merely the starter mechanism that had malfunctioned. I did a three engine take off, spooled up the relevant engine whose motor then engaged and flew back to Vigie in one piece on four engines.

St Lucia Airways was owned by a very interesting couple - Allison Skeete and Frank Von Wahl. Allison was a member of a St Lucian family who had made their money from banana production on the island and Frank was originally from Estonia. His town had twice been occupied by an invading foreign nation - Germany and then Russia - and he had decided to try his luck in Canada and, after obtaining an aeronautical degree, he was offered a job on St Lucia teaching aeronautics in a local technical college. Subsequently, he met Allison and, with his aviation knowledge, the two of them set up St Lucia Airways.

Getting paid once a month by Frank involved my camping out on his doorstep until the cash was finally presented in a variety of currencies - US Dollars, French Francs, British West Indies Dollars and Barbadian Dollars. My currency of choice was the French Franc since Martinique was just across the water so once a month on a trip to that island I'd convert all the cash into French travelers checks since there was no US territory within range and I didn't trust the other two currencies.

This idyllic lifestyle came to an end when my wife became pregnant and we decided that St Lucia was perhaps not the best place for childbirth. Not that there was anything wrong with native medicine on the island. An American, whom Nick had employed on board his yacht Cariad, had been electrocuted in the bilges of the yacht and his wound had turned gangrenous. But a local St Lucian went up into the mountains, plucked some leaves from a tropical plant, wrapped them around the wound and within 24 hours the gangrene had been cured.

Shortly after my wife's pregnancy, I was summoned by the Royal Naval Reserve (Air) Branch to Scotland to participate in a NATO exercise doing duty in the Operations Room at the Maritime Headquarters near Edinburgh before flying a single seat Hunter in another NATO exercise out of Aalborg in Denmark. Our perfect Caribbean life had to come to an end but it had been an enlightening and exciting experience and we had met and bonded with many fine people who were always smiling and happy although their lives were not nearly as fortunate as ours.

The flying was nothing if not different and the scenery was always scintillating. Nick was subsequently sadly killed in a game park jeep accident in South Africa and Pat moved back to the continent of her birth and now lives to the east of Cape Town. Allison and Frank subsequently sold St Lucia Airways and it was later in the news for all the wrong reasons when it was revealed that the new St Lucia Airways had been clandestinely ferrying arms in Boeing 707s for Oliver North and the CIA to Iran.

This was after Iraq had invaded Iran and the USA had supplied Iraq with ordnance, including chemical weapons. The Iran arms operation later became known as Contragate (as in Watergate) since the money generated by the sale of these weapons to Iran was used to fund the Contras in an attempt to dislodge the Sandinista Government in Nicaragua. Frank died some years ago but Allison still lives on St Lucia and plans are afoot for us to visit her again on her beautiful island. Life is full of surprises and never dull.

# Chapter 10

## Northern Indiana Supply Co, Reinsurance and the Royal Naval Reserve (Air Branch)

Northern Indiana Supply Company (NISCO) was founded in 1933 and specialises in Industrial Distribution. It's headquartered in Kokomo in Indiana and, in the past, had branches in Marion, Peru and Lafayette - all in Indiana. Currently, the head office remains in Kokomo with its only other branch in Marion.

When my time flying with St Lucia Airways and my temporary duty with the Royal Naval Reserve (RNR) Air Branch in Scotland and Denmark had been carried out, I was still on the books of British Airways (BA) back in London. However, out of the blue, my wife's brother-in-law, Terry, thought it would be a jolly wheeze to employ me in Marketing and Sales in NISCO's Marion office although I knew diddly squat about Industrial Distribution. Terry's father had started NISCO all those years ago and Terry was now the Chairman.

Lisa and I and our three kids moved to Marion, rented a house and settled into life in the Midwest which was a trifle different from our halcyon days in the Caribbean. With my future with BA uncertain, I thought it important for me to first obtain my US Air Transport Pilot's license (ATP) to go along with my British ATPL and my Windward Islands licence. To achieve this, I did a crash two day course in a hotel in Chicago to get up to speed for the ATP's written exam and three days later I took and passed this exam at the Federal Aviation Administration's (FAA) base at the Indianapolis Airport.

The ATP course teacher in Chicago was a laid off American Airlines pilot who instructed the class to ask no questions but instead to remember the answers to just about every question that had ever been asked in past exams. After two subsequent days spent studying the questions and answers, I was able to pass the written exam with a high mark although I suspect that, if I'd taken the exam a few days later, I would have forgotten it all and failed miserably.

I was then required to pass the ATP multi engine flight check which I did at South Bend Indiana airport on a two engine Cessna 310 after practising at a small airport in Angola Indiana. I never could land the Cessna 310 very smoothly on two engines but, luckily, my examiner on the day of my flight check was a charming retired airline pilot who insisted on acting as my co-pilot and he only required me to show him that I could carry out emergency single engine landings which didn't require a great deal of finesse. He never did ask me to make a two engined landing which I'm sure I would have bungled. I came away with my Multi Engine Rating which was a big relief.

It was now time for me to get to work with NISCO by learning the intricacies of industrial hardware such as Hoists and Cranes, Valves, Fittings, Cutting Tools, Hoses, Sprockets and Flanges etc and to steel myself to pay calls on the Purchasing Agents (PAs) at giant factories such as AC Delco, General Motors and General Tire in order to sell them this complicated equipment about which I knew very little. Amazingly, I was always greeted very warmly. I think these PAs felt extremely sorry that I, a clueless Brit, had been thrust in at the deep end and it helped that I played up my ignorance and always asked for their assistance in placing orders. Often, the PA would take me out to lunch when I, as the salesman, should have been treating them to a meal. I guess the English accent didn't hurt and everybody I met in all these large corporations always wanted to know what the devil I was doing in northern Indiana. Some of my aviation friends jokingly called me "The Flangeman". In addition to making many sales calls around northern Indiana, I was also sent on courses at Budgit Hoist in Muskegon, Michigan and Lunkenheimer Valve in Cincinnati, Ohio.

After a time, we decided to purchase a house in a very nice neighborhood in Marion as house prices - compared to the East Coast - were remarkably low and for next to nothing we were able to buy a four bedroom ranch style bungalow with a large yard and a finished basement. But, to be honest, Marion, with a population of around 30,000, was not the most exciting of towns but it did have a very nice golf club, Meshingomesia, over 30 churches and a good college – Marion College - where I attended a course in economics. It was also 85 miles from Indianapolis and 50 miles from Fort Wayne - two of Indiana's largest cities - so we had our escape routes - including being able to attend the Indy 500 auto race where my father-in-law had been a volunteer marshal. All in all, my time at NISCO was well spent and I certainly broadened my horizons and knowledge in a field that was unknown to me before we moved to the Midwest.

After two years of "sprockets and flanges", two events occurred which again changed our lives.

First, British Airways told me, and all the other pilots that they had put on furlough, that there were no piloting positions available but instead they were making us three offers. One was to move to London and work in Flight Operations at Heathrow Airport, the second was to convert to being a Flight Attendant (Steward) and the third was to take Early Retirement and be paid a tax free lump sum.

It was about this time that I also received a call from an old British fighter pilot acquaintance who was employed by a Reinsurance Broker at Lloyd's of London which specialized in Aviation.

This ex-pilot had set up an office for the London broker in Lower Manhattan in New York City but he now wanted to return to the UK. Would I be interested in taking over his position running this small company? Just like Industrial Distribution, I knew next to nothing about Reinsurance but I did know a little about Aviation. As a result, the decision to accept early retirement from British Airways and to take up this offer was an easy one and we moved to New Jersey and I started commuting to work in New York City - initially by train and then by car, ferry and eventually high speed catamaran.

At one stage, four of us commuters, who had flying licenses, toyed with the idea of leasing a float plane with retractable wheels and commuting to the East River in Lower Manhattan from either the Robbinsville or Princeton airports in New Jersey. However, we soon came to the realisation that the security of our plane might be in jeopardy if we left it tied up on the Hudson river all day close to the South Street Seaport and the crazy idea was soon shelved. The thought of returning to the plane after work and perhaps discovering that the propeller had been "borrowed" helped us with our decision.

Now is not the time to bore my readers with the subtle delights of Proportional, Non - Proportional and Facultative Reinsurance and Quota Shares, Excess of Loss and Reinstatement Premium Protections etc. Suffice it to say, I specialised in General Aviation - all Aviation excluding Airline exposures - and my business travels took me to Lloyd's of London and the London Company market, plus France, Germany, Switzerland, Bermuda and Australia. Twice, my trips Down Under coincided with Australia's richest horse race - the Melbourne Cup at Flemington racecourse - which I was able to attend on both occasions. Always held on the first Tuesday in November, this race is the handicap with the highest purse in the world and, being a public holiday, the entire nation comes to a grinding halt. Punters flock to the local betting parlors, families delight in holding auctions and sweepstakes to find the winner and a vast crowd swarms the racecourse itself dressed to the nines in what could be called a Southern Hemisphere Royal Ascot. One year, the first three horses home were all trained in Ireland so it really has become an important international sporting event.

I worked for five broking houses during my time in Reinsurance, including Bradstock, Jardine, Willis and Benfield - all companies that were headquartered in London although I worked for them in their offices in New York and for a brief period in New Jersey. The good news was that all of the senior executives at these broking houses in London were keen skiers, as I was, so I was required once a year to head to Europe to ski with clients at such as the Trois Vallees and Val d'Isere in France and Zurs and Lech in Austria. And, of course, five hours of boredom on the golf course was always deemed to be a good occupation for talking clients into buying even more reinsurance than they needed.

My clients were either Insurance Companies or Underwriting Agencies (who accepted risks on behalf of Insurance Companies) insuring Corporate jets, Private Aircraft and more esoteric equipment such as Crop Dusters in the Midwest and Seaplanes in Alaska. My role was to minimise the risks these insurance entities faced in the event of aviation losses by laying off the majority of their exposures into the secondary international reinsurance market. And the reinsurers who assumed these risks would, in turn, reinsure their liabilities by also buying reinsurance protections from international markets through a process that became known as the retrocessional spiral. Reinsurance is all about laying off risk - not unlike the actions of a bookmaker who hedges his bets with other bookies in the event that his book is too heavily loaded on the favorite.

I also had fun producing a monthly quiz based on non-Reinsurance Aviation questions which I sent out around the world. The first person with the highest number of correct answers won a case of champagne - some of which had to be drunk with me in New York City. Fortunately, my outlay was small as many winners were from Europe and even the thought of imbibing bottles of free bubbly could not justify them flying to New York to enjoy their prize. There was also the problem of differing time zones since Europe is normally five or six hours ahead of New York and eight or nine hours ahead of the West Coast. Sending the questions to the US markets after Europe had closed gave the English, French, Germans and Swiss a big disadvantage but, on the other hand, sending the questions out after all of the USA offices had closed put the European markets in the driving seat when their offices opened the next morning. And the time zone difference with Australia was far too large for me to satisfy all of the participants all of the time.

My many years in Reinsurance also involved my continuing duties as a fighter pilot with the Royal Naval Reserve (Air) Branch and so, once a year, I was able to arrange for a business trip to London to coincide with my month's duty flying a Hawker Hunter single seat jet fighter in the NATO exercise - Exercise Bold Game - out of Aalborg in Jutland on the mainland of Denmark. This annual duty required me to first present myself at Royal Naval Air Station (RNAS) Yeovilton in Somerset in the southwest of England. There I did a rush refresher flying course on the two seat Hunter T8 and practised liferaft and ejection seat drills before I flew with my squadron of single seat Hunter GA11s to Denmark. This was quite a remarkable experience as flying the Hunter was pretty much my only flying each year although I did occasionally rent a Cessna 172 which was a far cry from flying a fighter capable of attaining trans-sonic speeds, pulling up to 7Gs and firing rockets and dropping bombs.

Exercise Bold Game could not have been more fun as it involved carrying out dummy strikes on German Navy Fast Patrol Boats (FPBs), which would lurk in Norwegian fjords, before we refueled at Stavanger airport on the southwest corner of Norway. On the return to Aalborg, we would engage in simulated fighter combat with Danish Air Force F16s who would "bounce" us after we got airborne from Stavanger. Surprisingly, us Reservists in our ancient

Hunters came out remarkably well during our hassles with the newer Danish fighters - mainly because we employed sneaky tactics with our two ship formations. One tactic involved having one Hunter down at sea level as bait with its wing man sitting at 20,000 feet up in the sun and behind. Needless to say, the Danish F16s would attempt to pounce on the lower aircraft, which was easy to see, only for them to become the meat in the sandwich when the top Hunter screamed down from altitude to score a simulated kill on the Danes.

I became very friendly, and still am, with one of the Danish F16 pilots and, as we always had a two seat Hunter with us on the Exercise, I was able to take him up on a number of missions so he could see what "fighting" the F16 was like from the other side. Like many Danish military pilots, he subsequently joined their national airline - SAS - and for many years lived near Annecy in France and operated out of Geneva Airport. He is still a good friend.

One amusing interchange I heard one day on the emergency frequency on my Hunter aircraft's radio involved two Italian Air Force Fiat G91 fighters and the Hamburg Air Traffic Control Center. My wingman and I were flying close to German airspace to the north of Hamburg when a voice said over the air - "This is Hamburg Center - Two Fiat G91s who have just overflown Hamburg airport at high speed at 50 feet - please report your identity". To which one of the G91 pilots replied in accented English - "Ha Bloody Ha". Hamburg immediately retorted with the remarkable statement - "Two G91s - it will not be Ha Ha for you tomorrow". The two Italians had obviously got lost on a training mission and had blasted their way across Hamburg airport at a very low level.

During Bold Game, we also fired two inch rockets and dropped bombs in 20 degree dives on a bombing range in Jutland but this came to a halt when we managed to set fire to the range with our weaponry which naturally upset the Danish Air Force.

Bold Game was a very civilised Exercise since there was no flying at weekends. This gave us pilots time to explore the town of Aalborg and play tennis on the air base which incidentally had been the Nazis' largest in area military airfield during WWII. Aalborg was an interesting town as it always appeared to be totally dead on a Saturday afternoon but by 9 pm it was jumping and it stayed that way until the wee hours of the morning. Many late Saturday nights were spent with our Danish pilot friends crawling from bar to bar where the pop group "Foreigner" seemed to be the flavor of the moment.

I also visited Aarhus and Copenhagen and on a number of occasions my fellow pilots and I took the tiny one car train up to Hirtshals on the northern tip of Jutland. Hirtshals is the port town from where the ferries run across the Skagerrak to Oslo and other Norwegian ports and was where we discovered a very attractive tavern called the "Admiralen" - or Admiral's Inn. This tavern, which had a painting of an old English pub sign entitled the "Naval Reserve", was an appropriate watering hole for us nautical Reservists and the kitchen did us proud with delicious and lengthy Sunday lunches. The after lunch drink of choice was a nasty black concoction called Nord Zee Olie - North Sea Oil in English - which, being a cousin of schnapps, would readily encourage sleep on the train ride back to Aalborg.

My time as a Lieutenant Commander in the RNR Air Branch eventually came to an end and I took retirement after 12 years of service in the Reserves. And some years later, I decided I'd had enough of my many years of Reinsurance and quit my paid job to concentrate on the volunteer work I was now doing at home and abroad.

# Chapter 11

## Peace and Quakerism

---

As described in the previous chapter, after many years as an enthusiastic Naval fighter pilot, I left the military to fly with the airlines but was subsequently asked to join the Royal Navy Reserve (RNR) Air Branch. Although I was living in the USA, my British Reserve duties required me to don my uniform once a year when I would travel to England and on to Denmark to fly a single seat fighter in a NATO exercise in Scandinavia.

This can only be described as a boondoggle since I was paid as a Lieutenant Commander on flight pay from the day I set foot in England while receiving a per diem allowance for my time on duty. On top of that, I combined my duty with subsequent business at Lloyds of London as an aviation reinsurance broker and my New York company paid for the cost of my transatlantic flights as well as my normal broking salary during the course of my military duty. Screaming around the fjords of Norway at low level with my squadron while "attacking" German fast patrol boats, being jumped by Danish F16 fighters on my way back to base in Denmark and occasionally dropping bombs was all too much fun.

It was at this stage in my life that I started to question my role as someone who was trained to spread death and destruction around the world. This was very unsettling for me and I began searching for an answer.

During my time in the Reserves, I had become a member of the Princeton Officers Society (POS) which met for dinner on a regular basis at the Nassau

Club in Princeton New Jersey. However, I had already begun to realise more and more that what I had been doing in the military was contrary to the cause of peace and I was fortunate to get to know the first of four gentlemen who helped me to see the light and to become an ardent Peace Activist and subsequently a Quaker.

The Chairman of the POS was the Reverend Ernest Gordon - the Scottish retired Dean of the Princeton University Chapel - who had been a prisoner of war of the Japanese after Singapore had fallen in 1942. As an officer in the Argyll and Sutherland Highlanders, Ernest had escaped in a junk when Singapore fell - only to be picked up by a Japanese tanker within sight of India. He was forced to spend the rest of the war on the Burma Railroad and subsequently wrote a very moving book called "Through the Valley of the Kwai". In it, he describes how he found religion by helping fellow prisoners survive their ordeal - an ordeal compounded by the "dog eat dog" behaviour of many of his countrymen who stole other prisoners' medicine and food and in many ways caused more suffering than that carried out by the Japanese and Korean guards.

Upon demobilisation from the British Army in 1945, Ernest obtained a degree in theology from Edinburgh University, was given a Fellowship in the USA and ended up as the Dean of the Princeton University Chapel for 37 years. During the postwar years, he spent much time in Japan counselling the young about the horrors of the atomic bombing of Hiroshima and Nagasaki and in trying to educate the Japanese about the crimes against humanity which their country had committed prior to and during WWII. His example was a moving eye opener for me and I decided from then on to pursue a life in pursuit of peace. Coincidentally, four pilots in my F4 squadron at NAS Miramar in San Diego had been in the Class of '67 at Princeton University and they all subsequently spoke in awed tones about Dean Gordon.

Next, I was very fortunate to meet up with the Reverend Bob Moore - the esteemed long term Executive Director of the Coalition for Peace Action (CFPA) in Princeton. The wonderful example that Bob sets and his eloquent message soon convinced me to join the CFPA and I've been an active member for over 15 years. My recent experiences in a Syrian Refugee Camp in Greece and my time in Yemen in my military days have caused me to focus on Syria and Yemen where the United States has been sadly complicit in their destruction. I also demonstrate at the Drone Command Center which is outside the old NAS Willow Grove in Horsham Pennsylvania.

My membership of the CFPA involves Letters to the Editor, monthly meetings on Peace Education and Political Action, phone calls to our Congressmen, two visits a year to Congress to speak with Senators and Representatives on such issues as North Korea, Iran, Gun Violence, Syria, Drone warfare and Yemen and there is also a very special annual Multi Faith Service for Peace in the Princeton University Chapel each November followed by our Annual Conference.

Other highlights of the CFPA's agenda have included lunches and gatherings where the speakers have been such as Andrew Young, Dan Ellsberg, Noam Chomsky and Lawrence Wilkerson. I was the Reverend Jesse Jackson's personal handler when he preached the sermon at one of our Multi Faith Services and also spoke at the CFPA's Annual Conference. Many other highly respected individuals who have spoken at CFPA events feel, like we do, that slaughter and destruction are crimes against humanity and these crimes must be stopped if the world is to avoid a continuing cycle of destabilization and poverty with the killing of more and more innocent people. All these gatherings and events are led by our noble leader, Bob Moore, who promotes the cause of peace in a dignified and humble fashion which endears him to so many who are fortunate to get to know him and all that he stands for.

Sadly, the USA has been responsible for or influential in the death of over 20 million people since WWII in at least 37 countries and the CFPA is at the forefront of the many NGOs which are attempting to promote Diplomacy before War. As Winston Churchill once said "War is the Failure of Diplomacy" and "Jaw, Jaw, Jaw before War, War, War". The US complicity and involvement in the destruction of the Middle East and elsewhere is ongoing and this devastation must be stopped through all peaceful means possible.

From a personal viewpoint, I've spent time in and around the village of El Mozote in El Salvador where nearly 1,000 innocent "campesinos" were slaughtered in 1981 by the Salvadoran Army whose senior officers had graduated from the USA's School of the Americas. The State Department was complicit in these crimes against humanity and "The Massacre at El Mozote" by Mark Danner is a must read for anyone studying US Foreign Policy.

The next gentleman to influence me in the cause of peace and who introduced me to Quakerism was Bill Strong. Bill was a fellow member of the CFPA and a bookbinder and ironically I took my four military flying log books to him to be rebound - not knowing that he was a Quaker. Upon arrival at his house in Princeton, I noticed a board on his lawn which stated "War is not the Answer" alongside a Peace Dove sign. On meeting Bill, I soon learned that he was indeed a Quaker and I became eager to hear what he had to say about Quakerism. At that time, my knowledge of Quakerism was scant although I did know that peace was imperative to the Quaker faithful and that many Quakers had been conscientious objectors during World Wars I and II and also during the Vietnam war.

I met the fourth individual who influenced me in my conversion to Peace and Quakerism when I was tutoring in the Adult Education Program at the Trenton Area Soup Kitchen (TASK) - as I still do. I was very fortunate to get to know the amazing Dr Christian Hansen who had been a pediatrician to the poor in many countries around the world. He was a Quaker but although he attended a Quaker school - Haverford College - he did not come to Quakerism until later in life.

This enlightenment comes to many of us who are not "birthright" Quakers - i.e. born into a Quaker family - and Dr Hansen saw the light during the course of his superb work in poor communities - first on a Native American reservation and then in many struggling countries on the African continent. Sadly, Dr Hansen died a few years ago and his memorial service at the Buckingham Pennsylvania Friends (Quaker) Meeting House was attended by tutors and adult students from TASK and, being a Quaker meeting, many, who adored Christian, stood up and told us all what a great influence he had been in helping them improve their lives. Perhaps the highlight of the service was the moving eulogy that his adoring eldest son gave - not least because, at the end, he held up a photo of Christian standing on the South Rim of the Grand Canyon - naked except for a pair of hiking boots. This piece of frivolity and what I had learned about the Quaker philosophy from him and Bill convinced me that I too should become a Quaker. I had never been excited about organised religion and the Quaker practice of unprogrammed silent worship appealed to me in conjunction with my quest for peace.

The letters of the word SPICES best describe the message of Quakerism. S for Simplicity, P for Peace, I for Integrity, C for Community, E for Equality and S for Stewardship and I don't believe there are any plausible arguments against these qualities and I've been an active Quaker for a number of years.

First, I attended the Princeton Meeting and I now more often go to Crosswicks and Arneys Mount New Jersey although I have enjoyed a variety of many different Quaker gatherings having attended Meetings in Trenton, Greenwich, Quakertown, Mt Holly, Rancocas, Tuckerton, Barnegat - all in New Jersey - and in Hope Valley and Guildford in England, Toulouse in France and Cape Town in South Africa.

The original Quakers who first met in Crosswicks in the late 1600s came from the town of Chesterfield in Derbyshire in the north of England and that is the reason that Crosswicks sits in Chesterfield Township. Interestingly, Quakerism came to Cape Town - not from England where most American Quakers originally came from - but from the island of Nantucket. Nantucket was a Quaker whaling community and in the 1800s the Nantucket whalers headed south to the Southern Ocean in search of the southern right whale and, making Cape Town a last port of call for supplies, introduced Quakerism to the Cape.

With all my involvement in the Peace Movement and Quakerism, it's very ironical that, not long ago, I was presented with a medal by the Malaysian Consul General at his Consulate in New York City. The Pingat Jasa medal was awarded to those who had participated over 50 years ago in what became known as the Indonesian Confrontation which I mention in the Chapter entitled "East of Suez". This was at a time when Malaya was gaining its independence from Great Britain and Indonesia saw the opportunity to attempt to take over the Malayan peninsula and the island of Borneo. I was flying off the aircraft carrier Ark Royal and the Royal Navy, the British Army and a number of Commonwealth forces successfully prevented the Indonesians from carrying out their attempted invasion although they did manage to land a few paratroopers on the mainland and they fought very fiercely on Borneo.

At no time did I do anything that truly deserved a medal. The warm reception, medal presentation and lunch that I, and Lisa, received from the Consul General and his team in New York left a lasting impression and, being an ardent Quaker and Peace Activist, I was able to justify the receipt of this military honour since it was for services rendered many moons ago and long before I came to terms with the horrors of warfare and had decided to devote my life to the cause of Peace and Quakerism.

# Chapter 12

## AYACUCHO - In the Peruvian Andes

A yacucho sits at around 9,000 feet in the Andes about 250 miles southeast of the Peruvian capital, Lima. Founded nearly 500 years ago, in 1540, by the Spanish conquistador, Francisco Pizarro, it has a current population of approximately 180,000 and 33 churches, one for each year of Jesus' life.

It was here that Lisa and I volunteered with Cross Cultural Solutions (CCS) a few years ago - CCS being the organisation with whom I later worked in the Ritsona Refugee Camp in Greece which is the topic of a subsequent chapter.

We flew to Lima, arriving late in the evening, and met up with our fellow volunteers at the international airport where we hung out together to wait for the departure of our small puddle jumper which was due to leave at 5.00 am the next morning for the one hour flight to Ayacucho. Much to our surprise, our flight was suddenly removed from the Departures board with no indication as to whether it would depart at a later time. Just as we were all discussing our next course of action, Rudy, our Peruvian program manager, arrived at the airport having travelled all night by bus from Ayacucho after he had learned of the cancellation of our flight. Luckily, Rudy was able to pull some strings with the local airline and off we flew to Ayacucho. We later discovered that this flight was always cancelled if the number of booked passengers was below a certain minimum required level.

There were eight of us volunteers living in the same comfortable house in town where the excellent meals were cooked for us by Peruvian chefs with lunch being the main meal which we ate between morning and afternoon sessions at our volunteer positions.

Lisa worked in what is known in Quechua - the native language - as a Wawa Wasi, or "baby house", which was similar to a pre-school in the USA - albeit the language spoken by the kids aged two to five was Spanish not Quechua. The Head Teacher was known as Mama and Lisa became Mama Lisa and she taught the sweet children the alphabet and numbers and played many games inside and outside with them between classes and after lunch.

I taught English in a pleasant High School where the students all spoke Quechua and Spanish - many of whom having walked up to 10 miles each day through the mountains to get to school.

With my appalling Spanish and zero Quechua, I was blessed with a local teacher who was fluent in both languages. She knew little English but, with her help, I was able to improve the students' English as we covered grammar, spelling and even essay writing.

The classrooms were quite basic but there was an attractive vegetable garden where the students were encouraged to plant and cultivate crops with a view to taking them home once they had grown to edible size. During break, the students played soccer in the playground with stones or baseball caps being used to mark the goal posts and basketball and volleyball were also very popular although there was no netting for either sport - just the metal hoop for basketball and a line of rope for the volleyball net.

Teachers were required to personally provide all necessary books, tools and equipment for the classrooms and even copies had to be paid for by the teacher. Paperwork that required to be copied was taken by a student, with the teacher's cash in hand, to a small hut in the playground where a lady sat all day making copies at a cost not dissimilar to that charged in a local US library. The organisation in the school was pretty chaotic so I took it upon myself to plan my own curriculum - always in a different classroom - which appeared to be much appreciated. I was able to buy my teacher a number of necessary classroom supplies in the local market place but there was no netting available for basketball and volleyball in Ayacucho. Instead, on returning to the USA, I purchased the required nets and shipped them to the school.

Sadly, Ayacucho had been the starting point of the Sendero Luminoso (Shining Path) movement when a former professor at the local university -

Abimael Guzman - initially felt there was a need for some form of ideological action to counter the right wing government of Alberto Fujimori. Unfortunately, when peaceful results from his movement were not forthcoming, Guzman resorted to more violent tactics and the Sendero Luminoso turned to full scale guerrilla warfare resulting in massive bloodshed on both sides with nearly 70,000 deaths during the course of this devastating conflict. Both sides committed human rights atrocities but the Peruvian Government was responsible for a large majority of those killed - often innocent campesinos (peasants) who were unable to tell the Peruvian Army where guerrillas were hiding because they didn't know.

By the time we arrived in Ayacucho, all was peaceful and fighting had ceased. Guzman had been captured and is still in prison. Fujimori was subsequently jailed for his brutal tactics although he had been given a very unpopular pardon after returning from asylum in Japan. Because of the previous instability in Ayacucho, we were the only "gringos" in this lovely Spanish city and no tourists meant no picture postcards for sale.

In addition to our teaching roles, Lisa and I spent time in a medical clinic and also went further up into the mountains to a small village which had sadly seen more than its fair share of death and destruction during the civil war. We were asked to teach young kids in the village school which was very rewarding as the children were thrilled to leave their often one room huts where they lived with their parents and grandparents. Living in such close quarters with adults, sex education for the children was deemed a necessity and many explicit sex education picture books were on hand in the school for the students, some as young as three, to study.

Another interesting event took place one day at this little school which I think would have shocked the majority of parents in the USA. The village elders had decided that the community needed a higher quality of cow so all the kids were led outside at lunchtime to watch a large number of cows being artificially inseminated by a local veterinarian. I wonder whether a few lawsuits might ensue if kids were exposed to this performance in the USA?

One day, we were asked to spend time with children from the local women's prison. Their mothers, who lived high in the Andes, had been caught up in the initial stage of the cocaine chain whereby they were paid very little, but more than they normally earned, to convert coca leaves into paste for onward conversion to cocaine itself. This first step in the production of cocaine is illegal and the majority of the finished product is sold to customers abroad - much of it into the USA. At that time in Peru, children could remain with their mothers in prison up to the age of three and our role was to take the kids out of the prison for the day and play games with them in the local park and treat them to ice cream and other tasty delights.

The women's side of this prison was very clean which could not be said for the men's section where the inmates lived in squalid conditions and fighting appeared to be very prevalent. The women spent their days making garments from the wool of the alpaca - the alpaca being a domesticated vicuna which is an indigenous Andean animal not unlike a small llama. These garments were then sold by volunteers outside the prison - and often into the USA - with the proceeds being returned to the inmates and their families. Not long ago, a Danish startup company named Carcel, (Spanish for Prison) commenced selling these garments through the internet.

Apart from trying to assist with educating the children in and around Ayacucho, we too were educated and this included Spanish lessons, the history of Peru, the development of Cocaine and the mysteries of Native Medicines. We legally chewed coca leaves and drank coca tea - both antidotes for altitude sickness - and our teacher, a professor at the university, also performed some mind reading on us with the use of coca leaves. First, we were each asked to think of a secret question which we were not to reveal to the professor and then to select five pristine coca leaves which we squeezed between our hands before dropping them onto a table.

Amazingly, my question to myself was whether I would volunteer with CCS again. Without knowing what my question was, the professor studied my leaves and immediately told me I would do volunteer work abroad again - which indeed I did do in both Cape Town and in the Syrian refugee camp in Greece with CCS.

Regarding the thousand year old practice of native medicines, it was very surprising that the starfish was used as a cure for ailments since there aren't too many starfish at 9,000 feet in the Andes. But the most amazing native medicinal practice is the use of a live guinea pig to diagnose mental illnesses known as "pachua" in Quechua. Although the guinea pig is a local culinary delicacy, a live guinea pig is also rubbed over the head of a mentally ill patient and then vivisected (cut open while still alive) and the innards examined. This extraordinary technique supposedly allows a successful diagnosis to be made. Presumably the poor animal is then subsequently devoured at dinner that night. Many of the flat roofed houses have guinea pig runs where these little animals are bred and often locals with wheelbarrows full of alfalfa are to be seen in the streets of Ayacucho since the guinea pig thrives on this green vegetable. I did eat guinea pig - but only once - as it tasted like very greasy chicken and I wasn't too happy about the practice of vivisection.

At weekends, we were free to roam Ayacucho with its stunningly beautiful old Spanish buildings and every Sunday there was always some form of military parade with exotic bands and soldiers dressed in their colorful uniforms. We spent two days one weekend exploring various small villages in the mountains and stayed in a very basic inn where there appeared to be a black market for toilet seats. As in many other bathrooms in and around Ayacucho, the toilet seats were missing - perhaps having been sold abroad to countries where these seats are in short supply?.

The highlight of our time away from Ayacucho was a weekend trekking in the Andes with a guide named Pancho who rented llamas for us to carry our backpacks and who led us over a mountain pass to a small farm at around 12,000 feet where we camped for the night. After an excellent cooked supper eaten in the farm's open courtyard, we retired to our tents for what turned out to be a rather unsettled night. Lisa and I initially shared a tiny two person tent in the farmyard but my incessant snoring drove her out - to sleep in a van with a number of Pancho's cohorts who had driven the van up to the farm from the other side of the pass. Needless to say, their combined snoring was worse than mine - not to mention a continual surfeit of flatulence. Meanwhile, I slept soundly alone in my little tent until a rooster standing outside the tent - probably only four inches from my head - let rip with his morning serenade as the sun came up giving me the fright of my life.

All in all, our time in Ayacucho was an amazing experience among charming people in a quintessentially ancient Spanish city whose bucolic center, with its fountains and flocks of pigeons, had in no way been despoiled by modern commercialism - such as neon signs and vulgar billboards.

# Chapter 13

## CAPE TOWN - KHAYELITSHA and LANGA
## Townships, South Africa

---

Khayelitsha and Langa are two of the many Townships on the Cape Flats to the east of Cape Town in the Western Cape of South Africa. It was there that Lisa and I taught school after our stimulating experiences teaching in Ayacucho in the Peruvian Andes. We decided to offer our services again to Cross Cultural Solutions (CCS) with whom we had both been in Peru and with whom I subsequently volunteered in the Ritsona Refugee Camp in Greece.

As I had spent some of my childhood in Simon's Town, about an hour south of Cape Town on False Bay, going back to South Africa was like a homecoming for me although the Black and Coloured Townships, where we taught, are a far cry from a genteel and sadly whites only town such as Simon's Town where I had lived as a boy.

There are over three million people living in abject poverty in the Townships of which approximately 95% are Black with the remainder being Coloured or of Asian descent. The Blacks are mainly Xhosa and Zulu while the Coloureds are mostly descendants of the slaves from India, the Persian Gulf and even China who were brought to the Cape by the original Dutch settlers. Many of the Coloureds in the Townships are Muslim but a number of Muslims also live in the lovely Bo Kaap area in central Cape Town where there is the oldest mosque in South Africa - Auwal - built in 1794 - and delightful stone houses which are painted in a multitude of colours. The Townships are a legacy of the Apartheid era when the Group Areas Act forced many Blacks and Coloureds out of their traditional homes and into the flat wastelands to the east of the city.

Lisa taught English Writing, Reading Comprehension, Life Skills and Physical and Sex Education to 7th and 8th Graders with a teacher called Gladys in the oldest Township – Langa - which, founded in 1927, means "Sun" in Xhosa. Langa, near Gugulethu, is one of the smaller Townships with a population of around 50,000 whereas Khayelitsha (meaning "Our New Home"), where I taught, housed more than 300,000 Blacks and Coloureds. The living accommodation in these townships consists of cramped wooden huts, no paved roads, nor running water and there is approximately one outdoor toilet per 50 families. An interesting facet of the Townships is that nothing is recycled since every container, piece of equipment or trash is used again in some form or other as supplies are negligible and the average annual salary is the Rand equivalent of around $1,500. Amazingly, even cargo containers from the docks find their way to Khayelitsha where they are very popular as hairdressing salons and shops. Cooking is done on outdoor barbecues using natural wood and, with no cars (nor even bicycles), the Townships' carbon footprint is minimal.

My school in Khayelitsha was comparatively modern and clean and the kids all walked to school in their tidy blue and white uniforms. The majority of the students were very excited to come to school where they were fed a midday meal called "mealies" (a stew made from corn) and had a chance to play with other kids on the dirt playground as well as attend classes. Empty coloured plastic bottles were stuck in the ground around arid flower beds in the playground which enhanced the sparseness of the surroundings.

I taught three different classes of 40 kids in each class with the grade being known as 6th Grade which bore little resemblance to the US Grade system as my kids were aged anything from 11 to 16. These classes had a Xhosa teacher - Zuki - who showed little interest in teaching and who, fortunately, handed over the teaching responsibilities to me and rarely showed up in the classroom.

I was asked to teach a wide variety of subjects including Meteorology, Navigation/Map Reading, Geography, English Grammar, Poetry, Global Climate Change, Deforestation of the Rain Forests and even TV Script Writing. There were few lesson plans available but, through prior self study and winging it on the day, I was able to impart some of my knowledge on these varied subjects to the mostly very interested students.

The students spoke Xhosa and some English (but no Afrikaans which I had learned as a child as a young boy in South Africa but had mostly forgotten) so I was able to muddle through and I struck up a wonderful relationship with the majority of the kids. When I left to go back to the USA, one class presented me with beautiful handwritten cards and a bead necklace they had made in the South African colours. This was so moving that I had a hard time holding back the tears and the kids hung on to me with such compassion that my precious necklace, which I was now wearing, was broken although I was able to get it fixed upon return to the USA.

Early one Friday morning, Zuki, my delinquent teacher whom I hadn't seen all week, appeared in the doorway of my classroom and told me that she was going home for the weekend and that I was to teach Deforestation of the Rainforests on the coming Monday. On asking for a lesson plan on this topic, I was told that there wasn't one and so I went back to our accommodation and printed out information from my computer for me to teach with on Monday. On asking Zuki early on Monday morning for copies for the kids, she told me there was a paper shortage and she was only allowed to make one copy of each page. On top of that, these meagre copies could not be handed back to me until the next day. I played it by ear on the chalkboard and never did understand these paper rules - especially since every teacher's office was littered with reams of paper scattered on desks and on the floor.

The subject of Global Climate Change was received with great interest by the students - surprising as their carbon footprint was so small - and one little girl asked me if it would improve the situation if she planted a tree which of course in one small way it would. But whether she could afford to buy even a small tree was another matter.

After a few weeks, I asked each student in one of my classes to tell me what they wanted to do/be when they left school - and perhaps even college. Some of them would indeed obtain grants to go to the excellent University of Cape Town but the majority would sadly never move on from their depressing lifestyles in the Townships. Their desires for their futures after school were very stimulating but unlikely to be achievable - with Judge, Pop Star, Pilot, Naval Officer, Actor/Actress, TV Host, Doctor, Journalist being among their favorites. One girl, having learned that I had been a career pilot, would ask me every day how she could obtain her Pilot's Licence and how much it would cost - a cost sadly way outside what she would be able to afford.

Lisa and I lived with a small number of other international volunteers in a nice old house in the Cape Town suburb of Rosebank - a large house built in the 1840s - and we were driven each day to our assignments by Kimi, who was Coloured, and James, an Afrikaner. The other volunteers were not teaching but worked in clinics and hospitals and one of them, a lovely Indian girl called Tina, became a close friend and Lisa and I subsequently attended her bi-national wedding in Texas to a charming Iranian gentleman.

During the day, our house was full of a variety of staff who cleaned and cooked and helped run our programs. The head of the house, Luann, a white South African lady, was married to a Zulu and the other staff were Black, Coloured and Afrikaner and we ate our meals together in a delightfully cosmopolitan atmosphere where a wide variety of stimulating topics were discussed and traditional South African dishes such as Bobotie were consumed - Bobotie being curried mince meat topped with a milk and egg mixture.

In addition to our assignments, we too were educated - on the history of South Africa, the Xhosa language, how to play tribal drums and on the severe AIDs crisis by a lady with HIV. We were also taken to the Slave Museum in Cape Town where Kimi, our Coloured driver, proudly sat on a bench marked "Slegs Blankes" (Whites only) - a relic from Apartheid days. Cape Town is a delightful city with an ancient Castle, the Company's Gardens (so named because it was the brainchild of the Dutch East India Company) and one of the most exotic botanical gardens in the world - Kirstenbosch - with an amazing array of plants and trees including a vast number of protea - the national flower of South Africa.

At weekends, we were free to roam and we explored the Greenmarket, the food hall called the Old Biscuit Factory and Bo Kaap in Cape Town. Lisa climbed Table Mountain and Lion's Head (not me as I was suffering from osteoarthritis which was soon to be cured with a hip replacement) and we had the finest calamari ever at the Chapman's Peak Hotel on the west coast of Cape Town. We also attended two plays at the University of Cape Town's theatre in Stellenbosch by the renowned South African playwrights - Athol Fugard and J.M. Coetzee. The food and wine in the Cape Town area were second to none and remarkably cheap with the rate of exchange being 9 Rand to the Dollar. It's now even more attractive for US visitors being approximately 13 Rand to the Dollar.

The days of Apartheid are thankfully over and the population of Cape Town is now approximately 42% Coloured, 39% Black, 16% White, 1% Asian/Indian and 2% other nationalities. Apartheid is an Afrikaans word meaning "Aparthood" or "Separateness" and, while Nelson Mandela was able to improve the lives of so many South Africans after the collapse of Apartheid in the late 1980s, sadly conditions for many declined after his death but the resignation of the corrupt President, Jacob Zuma, led to some improvement under the current President, Cyril Ramaphosa, although Cape Town did suffer from a massive water shortage.

One morning was spent in the outdoor market in Hout Bay on the west side of Cape Town and afterwards Lisa and I took a "shared" taxi back to Cape Town which was an experience in itself. Sitting in the back row, we were sure that there wasn't room for more than the current 15 occupants but the taxi often stopped along the way and, at the final stop, a very large gentleman squeezed in next to us - much to our discomfort. One of the occupants was Marshal, the "guard", who collected the very cheap fares from the riders so that the driver could concentrate on his job and time would not be lost at the many pick up points along the way. For this duty, Marshal was able to ride free to see his family on a regular basis who lived some way away to the north of Cape Town. Many of the riders were mothers carrying their babies on their backs whose little heads always seemed to get banged on the top of the door when the mother was getting out of the van.

This "shared" taxi experience was a big contrast to the afternoon tea we subsequently had that day at the very grand Mount Nelson Hotel in Cape Town where staff in white jackets waited on us hand and foot. The Mount Nelson had been the British Army's senior officers' HQ during the second bloody Boer War in the late 1800s. A war that included the creation of concentration camps by the British and which resulted in British dominance in South Africa.

A friend of ours was one of the top racehorse trainers in South Africa with a training center at the old racecourse called Milnerton and we visited his stables on a couple of occasions but unfortunately we were not able to attend a weekend race meeting at the current race course - Kenilworth - to see his horses run because of cancellation of the races due to the weather.

Cape Town is the same distance south of the Equator as Atlanta Georgia is to the north of it but being surrounded by the Atlantic, Southern and Indian Oceans the weather can be quite unpredictable although a strong southwesterly wind known as the "Cape Doctor" often blows with supposedly healthy qualities. Our Afrikaner driver, James, was hooked on horse racing and, when he learned that I was a friend of one of the top trainers, he was all over me for tips - some of which did come to fruition.

We also spent a weekend exploring game parks with a Zulu guide and a small group of cosmopolitan visitors - including two from Angola. This weekend included visiting a rescue game park where we came in touching contact with elephants and saw cheetahs, leopards and a whole host of other wild animals. We stayed the night near the old Dutch town of Oudtshoorn where we fed ostrich and subsequently visited the towns of Paarl and Stellenbosch in the wine country. The sweetest town of all was Franschhoek, settled by French Huguenots and meaning French Corner in Afrikaans, with its thatched roofs, vineyards and stunning mountainous scenery. We also made the trip along the coast to Hermanus which is famous for its breaching southern right whales which we were fortunate to see.

As a Quaker, I was thrilled to discover that there was a Quaker Meeting House in Mowbray, next to where we were living in Rosebank, and I twice attended the multicultural First Day (Sunday) Meeting there comprising English, South Africans, Afrikaaners, Blacks and Coloureds. I had assumed that Quakerism had reached the Cape directly from England, as it had in America, but South African Quakerism came from the island of Nantucket off the coast of Massachusetts. Many of the Nantucket whalers were Quakers and Cape Town was their last port of call in the 1800s when heading south towards the Antarctic to hunt the southern right whale. Quakerism was introduced to Cape Town during their lengthy stopovers for provisions.

After our time in the Townships was over, my sister joined us from England and we rented a house in Simon's Town so we could revisit our old haunts from our days as kids. Simon's Town is a lovely small town on the sea - the home of the South African Navy - and is named after the original Dutch Governor, Simon van der Stel, and is also home to the famous penguin colony at Boulders Beach. We also explored the Cape of Good Hope which we learned is not the southernmost tip of the African Continent - that honour going to Cape Agulhas further to the east. And we were fortunate to gain access to the house my sister and I had lived in as children - Admiralty House - and where, as mentioned earlier, I had learned to ride my bike on our large lawn and to swim from our private beach. The access to our old home was through a South African friend who was Head of the Simon's Town Historical Society and whose daughter is now a real estate broker living near Princeton New Jersey. It's nothing if not a small world.

Although teaching in the Black Townships may not be for everyone, it proved an immensely rewarding experience for us and I highly recommend a visit to the Cape for anyone who wishes to enjoy fine food and wine, charming people, stunning scenery, sweeping beaches, fascinating game parks and perhaps even a rugby or cricket match or a horse racing meeting. Cape Town is at the very top of our list of all the cities we've been fortunate enough to visit during our time in many countries in the world.

# Chapter 14

## Plan International – Bolivia, El Salvador and Nicaragua

---

Pan International, originally known as Childreach, was founded in Spain in 1937 during the Spanish Civil War by two Englishmen - John Langdon-Davies, a journalist, and Eric Muggeridge, a relief worker - who both realised the need to provide support for homeless children during that devastating civil war. Spanish children were suffering in cities, such as Guernica, as a result of the death and destruction being wrought by Francisco Franco's Nationalist forces with the aid of the German Nazi and Italian Fascist air forces which had annihilated many Spanish cities. Plan's name subsequently morphed into Foster Parents Plan for Children in Spain and eventually into Plan International after being known as Foster Parents Plan for War Children during WWII. The concept for Plan was to provide aid by helping finance healthcare, water, sanitation, education, clothing, livestock and nutrition for children and their families and also for their communities..

Over 30 years ago, I became involved with this program when I sponsored a boy, Yamadou Traore, in Mali, the ex French colony in West Africa which is sadly in today's news for all the wrong reasons. Mali had been known as the French Sudan until gaining independence from France in 1960 - the year when many other French colonies in West Africa also gained their independence. When considering sponsoring children through Plan, I had decided to initially choose children in countries on the African Continent that I was not familiar with. As I had cousins in Kenya and Zambia in East Africa and had lived in

South Africa, the ex French colonies on the western side of Africa seemed a good choice for me.

At the same time that I took on Yamadou in Mali, I also sponsored a girl in Senegal, named Ndaye Mbombe, who lived not far from Senegal's capital Dakar and close to the old railroad line that still runs from Bamako, the capital of Mali, to Dakar. Senegal is another ex-French colony which also gained its independence in 1960. I had always intended to visit both families on a trip to that part of West Africa.

Yamadou and his family lived close to the Guinea border about 200 km up the Niger River from Bamako (City of Crocodiles in English) and the only means of transportation to get to his village was either by pinnace - a flat bottomed ferry - or by pirogue - not unlike a motorised canoe.

My original intention had been to fly with our young son to Bamako from the USA and travel up the Niger river to Yamadou's village but the trip to Bamako from New York required that we had to first fly to Amsterdam on KLM and then on to Bamako on Air Afrique. However, Yamadou's father was very elusive and rarely at home as he was often away hunting for gold in dry river beds and I didn't want to visit Yamadou unless all his family were there. I felt it important to meet them all and I had learned that I would be able to communicate with his family through an interpreter who spoke the local language, Bambara, and also French. Our son was the same age as Yamadou and they had become pictorial pen pals at the same time that a local social worker would also send letters to me. These letters were dictated by Yamadou's mother in Bambara to the social worker and then translated into archaic French with grammar dating back to the time that France had colonised Mali in 1890. I could just about get the gist of these letters with my schoolboy French.

I subsequently learned that Ndaye's family in Senegal, who were nomadic, had departed the Plan area and so my intention to see both kids on the same trip had to be shelved. My intended itinerary had been to take the steam train from Bamako to Dakar, after first seeing Yamado, and then to disembark at a small station near where Ndaye lived. But this was not to be after Ndaye's family upped and left and Yamadou outgrew the program at age 18.

Instead, I turned my attention to the Himalayan country of Nepal in Asia where I sponsored a young boy named Nihe who lived not far from Kathmandu.

Unfortunately, my relationship with Nihe and his family did not last long as his village was soon overrun by Maoist guerrillas and the family fled to a safe haven and I sadly lost contact with them.

It was now time to come closer to home so I took on a girl, Isela, in Nicaragua and another girl, Maybelline, in El Salvador - both countries I had never visited. Isela and her extended family of parents, aunts, uncles and cousins all lived in a jungle compound outside the beautiful old ex-Spanish city of Leon and I was able to visit them before Isela graduated from the program at age 18 and achieved a place at university. This was an amazing success story for a young girl living in very basic conditions and I stayed in Leon and spent two very happy days with her delightful family who treated me with the utmost warmth and fed me delicious meals in their dirt floored outdoor "dining room". I also spent a day in Isela's school and was most impressed with the dedication of her teachers and the reception given me by all the staff and the students who put on a dancing performance in my honour.

Leon, dating back about 500 years, is a lovely city and I enjoyed my time off by exploring its delights and also hiking in the nearby mountains. I also hooked up with two Basques and the three of us, with a guide, staggered up an active volcano - Cerro Negro (Black Hill in English) - with sand boards strapped to our backs. After arriving exhausted at the top of this peak, we then "volcano boarded" down the side of the mountain on the black lava. I sat discreetly on my board while my erstwhile Basque friends decided to stand which resulted in a number of falls causing nasty abrasions on their exposed skin as they were only wearing shorts.

I also stayed in the city of Granada - another delightful old Spanish city - and I came away with a great fondness for Nicaragua which is fast becoming the new Costa Rica although it is not as peaceful as the latter country which has had no military since 1948.

After visiting Isela in Nicaragua on this trip, I also took the long distance bus from Managua, the capital of Nicaragua, through Honduras, on the ten hour ride to San Salvador, the capital of El Salvador, in order to spend time with Maybelline and her family. I also visited El Salvador again to see Maybelline for a second time and so I got to know her and her family and school very well. Maybelline graduated from the program when she reached the age of 18 but my two visits to see her gave me a wonderful understanding of this beautiful but unstable country. Maybelline was a very bright young girl who was computer savvy and she did brilliantly with her studies and I spent time in her school where I donated baskets for the school's basketball court whose hoops lacked any form of netting - similar to my school in Ayacucho in Peru.

Maybelline and her family lived in a small community called El Morro (Morro is a type of tree) outside San Salvador. Their simple house was at the bottom of a small ravine and was built by Maybelline's father - the first house in the area to be built of concrete. It was also the only house to have an indoor toilet and a shower - albeit that the shower was built over the toilet! Perhaps the reason for this was to save water or to allow two functions to be performed at the same time?

Maybelline's father was a boiler mechanic and extremely practical. He designed a hydraulic system to move water up the ravine without using electricity so that all the families in the community had water for irrigation, cooking and washing. In addition to building their house, he also constructed an excellent outdoor open kitchen/dining area where all cooking was done on wood stoves and where I enjoyed excellent meals with the family.

In addition to spending time in Maybelline's school, I was able to hike in Walter Deininger Parc Nacional by the Pacific Ocean, eat many delicious pupusas and visit the province of Morazan in the northeast corner of El Salvador. I stayed in the small town of Perquin in Morazan near the Honduran border and close to the village of El Mozote where a ghastly massacre by the Atlacatl division of the Salvadoran Army took place in 1981. Many of the senior officers in the Salvadoran army were trained in the USA at the School of the Americas and sadly the United States was complicit in this appalling event at a time when the Reagan Administration was propping up right wing dictatorships in both Central and South America due to an exaggerated fear of Communism.

Close to 800 innocent men, women and children were slaughtered in El Mozote and adjoining villages and the United States has never come totally clean about the support given to the Salvadoran Army through training, weapons, advisers and intelligence. I made the pilgrimage to El Mozote and the village is now a sad memorial to the dead - all innocent peasants who were in no way aiding and abetting the left wing guerrilla movement known as the FMLN (Farabundo Marti Liberation National Front) which was fighting the Salvadoran Army.

Ironically, the current democratically elected governing party in El Salvador is an offshoot of the FMLN - not unlike the situation in Nicaragua which is now governed by the Sandinista party which the United States had tried to destroy by financing the Contra rebels through the illegal sale of ordnance to Iran in what became known as the Iran-Contra scandal. An excellent but distressing book - "The Massacre at El Mozote" by Mark Danner - is a must read for anyone interested in this despicable period in US foreign policy.

I stayed in a lovely inn in Perquin owned by a Mennonite from Delaware who had first come to that part of Central America to volunteer in refugee camps in Honduras when the civil war was raging in El Salvador in the early 1980s. In addition to running his excellent inn, he had also opened a very successful school where I spent some time and he developed an amazing hydroponic watering system using water from a lake to grow vegetables - with the water circulating from and back into the lake so there was no waste of this precious commodity. I've tried to help him open another school but the current situation in El Salvador, with its gang warfare, is not conducive to international support.

In addition to Maybelline in El Salvador, I have also sponsored a boy - Deimar - on the altiplano (high tableland) in Bolivia about two hours from the capital La Paz. It's certainly a small world as I was leading a historical walking tour in Princeton for the Historical Society of Princeton a few years ago when I learned that two of my "clients" were from Bolivia. I told them that I sponsored a boy in Bolivia and was planning to visit him in the not too distant future. Although I had only been with them for 20 minutes, they insisted that I must stay with them in La Paz when I came to Bolivia and that they would also pick me up at the airport. Sure enough, there they were when I landed at 13,000 feet in La Paz at two am one morning on my trip to see Deimar and I spent the next week in their charming guest accommodation on the grounds of their attractive house.

Deimar lived at 12,000 feet in a one room house with his parents, his grandparents and his sister with her small child. The family survived on subsistence arable farming but they did own a few pigs and cows and also guinea pigs which, similar to Peru, are considered delicacies. Deimar was a delightful young man with an avid appetite for reading and history. He walked to and from school each day and played and followed football (soccer) with a passion. I tried to persuade him to let me take him to a professional football match to see his favorite team, Bolivar, play in La Paz but he had never left his home in the mountains and was very uncomfortable at the thought of visiting a large city.

Local Plan staff always coordinated my visits with my families in El Salvador, Nicaragua and Bolivia which made communication much easier for me with my feeble Spanish. However, my other personal explorations in El Salvador, Nicaragua and Bolivia were always made on my own and at no time did I ever feel uncomfortable about what I was up to.

After my time with Deimar, my Bolivian hosts showed me much of La Paz and one day we drove from the city into the snow-covered Andes and down into the Amazon rainforest which gave me a great insight into the ecological diversity of this part of South America.

I was also able to take a side trip to Lake Titicaca which borders Bolivia and Peru and which is deemed to be the highest navigable lake in the world at 12,500 feet. Perhaps the highlight of my Bolivian trip, in addition to spending time with Deimar and his family, was climbing to the top of what was once the highest ski area in the world. Chacaltaya, at 17,785 feet, has sadly suffered from the effects of global climate change and no longer offers lift served skiing although base housing and the lift pylons are still in existence.

I hooked up with a Frenchman and some Brazilians and we headed out of La Paz in a rented shuttle and wound our way up the Andes to Chacaltaya's base area. We then started the long climb to the summit which I eventually reached - although some time after my younger companions had done so. I had once been to 16,000 feet in the Hindu Kush in Pakistan but this was my personal non-aviating altitude record - never to be done again.

After Maybelline and Deimar outgrew Plan's program, I took on one more child - a little girl named Sandri-Liliana in Cartagena in Colombia whom I hope to visit in the not too distant future. Plan International had led Lisa and me to Cross Cultural Solutions (CCS) with whom we volunteered in Peru and South Africa and I subsequently worked in the Ritsona Refugee Camp in Greece which is the subject of the next chapter.

# Chapter 15

## Ritsona Refugee Camp – Greece

A few years ago, I flew on Turkish Airlines to volunteer for two weeks with Cross Cultural Solutions (CCS) in the Ritsona Refugee Camp about an hour north of Athens. My journey took me first to Istanbul where I changed planes for the short flight to Athens. Turkish Airlines is one of the most popular airlines in the world and the service was impeccable and the food and wine both free.

I arrived in Athens late on a Friday night and took a taxi to the small coastal town of Mati to the east of Athens where I had made a reservation for the night. It turned out that my room, which the hotel had allocated for me, had a plumbing problem. With no other room available, the owner of the hotel kindly drove me in his car, at no charge, to a four star hotel on the water where I slept in an excellent room for my original price of 59 euros (approximately $67). This rate included a tasty cooked breakfast the next morning on the patio overlooking the bay.

I had been instructed to meet the other members of my eight person team of volunteers at the Arrivals Hall at Athens airport at 11.00 am the next morning. I duly hooked up with the seven ladies and Mohamed from Morocco who worked for CCS in Rabat but who was now going to be in charge of the CCS program in Greece for the rest of the summer. Also meeting us was Constantina, a young Greek girl employed by CCS, which meant we would have both an Arabic and a Greek speaker working with us.

All eight of us volunteers were alumni of various CCS programs with Lisa and I having been with CCS in Ayacucho in the Peruvian Andes and in Cape Town in South Africa. CCS, founded in 1995, had volunteer programs in eight countries and the eight of us were the first CCS volunteers to come to Greece to help out at Ritsona - a disused Greek Army Base. There were approximately 750 Syrian refugees of which a number were Kurds and a few other refugees from Iran and Somalia. We stayed in a hotel in Chalkida on the island of Evia which is about an hour north of Athens on the east coast and about 20 minutes from the Ritsona Camp. Chalkida is a 3,000 year old town - once called Chalkis - ancient Greek for copper which had been mined there many centuries ago. Being the only man in our group, I was fortunate to have my own room in the John's Hotel and we had breakfast in the hotel and supper in a nearby restaurant while CCS provided packed lunches for us at the Camp. Luckily, there was a Kurd at Ritsona who cooked delicious falafel and kebabs on an open fire which made for a pleasant alternative to the usual boring lunchtime sandwich.

After a Sunday of briefings and orientation, we started work at the Camp on the Monday morning and helped out in the Camp from 10.00 am to 4.30 pm each day, Monday to Friday, in stifling heat as the temperature often reached 100F with one day the thermometer actually hitting 109F.

Whereas IOM (International Organisation for Migration) and UNHCR (United Nations High Commissioner for Refugees) are the international inter-governmental bodies involved with refugees worldwide, Ritsona had a number of specific NGOs from various countries and we were assigned to work with Light House Relief - a Swedish organisation who had been at the Camp for approximately two years. Our CCS team were all from the USA but Light House had volunteers from Australia, New Zealand, France, Finland, England and the USA which made us a very international bunch.

Our roles were varied with some working with older women in what was known as the Female Friendly Space (FFS) and some in the Child Friendly Space (CFS) for young children below the age of six. Initially, I was with three others organising and conducting a Summer Camp with Light House from 1.00 pm to 4.00 pm for Syrian children aged approximately six to ten but, after a few days, I was moved to an older group of refugees aged 15 to 25. This group spent a lot of their time in the Youth Engagement Space (YES) and being with adult refugees was much more up my street. I thoroughly enjoyed our discussions about politics and their erratic journeys to Greece and I often talked about history and geography with them and played a number of quiz games and conundrums. At Ritsona, approximately 50% of the refugees were below 16 years of age while few were older than 55. I was thrilled with the knowledge that the young men I worked with demonstrated and with their eagerness to learn about the world in general. I did not see any young refugee women in the YES during my time at Ritsona.

I also sat in on English classes given by an excellent American high school teacher from California who was volunteering with the Swedish NGO - "I Am You". One class, attended by Syrians, Iranians and Somalis, centred on all the English words they would likely come across at airports - locations which would feature strongly in their lives if they were to achieve the necessary clearance to leave Greece. There were three women in the English class (two Somalis and one Iranian) but, other than these friendly ladies, I saw very few women in the Camp since they appeared to spend most of each day in their air conditioned accommodations and many refugees of both sexes slept well into the late morning.

A group from the pharmaceutical company Eli Lilly, in Indianapolis, coincided with us for our first three days as they had had a bad experience with safety issues in Jordan and were looking to see if Ritsona could benefit from their skills and altruism.

Most of my contacts at Ritsona were Syrians of whom many were Kurds and I also got to know a few Iranians. One 21 year old Syrian Kurd told me in great detail how he had escaped conscription into the Syrian Army just before his 18th birthday and had headed across the border into Kurdish Turkey. From there, he headed into Iraq but had to escape back into Turkey for fear of being captured by ISIS. In Turkey, he worked as a barman for a year before finding a smuggler to get him across the Aegean Sea to one of the official Greek refugee islands. From there, he was transported by Greek Government vessel to Chalkida and then on to Ritsona to be reunited with his mother and sister who had also found their way to Greece. His father was still in Syria in a village surrounded by ISIS which made his escape almost impossible.

One young adult refugee was very friendly but did not want to talk about his escape from Syria which was fully understandable - his condition being similar to those who have suffered from what is now known as PTSD after serving in combat in such as WWII and in Vietnam. Originally known as "shell shock", many who suffer from it never want to talk about their wartime experiences.

Another refugee from Iran told me that he was leaving in a few days for Lausanne in Switzerland as his immigration papers had finally come through but he never did leave the Camp as his means of air transportation had fallen through. He was one of the students attending the English classes with his brother and I was delighted when they invited me to have a cup of tea with them in their small Iso Box trailer which they shared with two others. Being invited to drink tea with them was quite symbolic and an honour and I saw it as a symbol of their respect for me. Their accommodation was small with four bunk beds but it did have a kitchen, a shower and a toilet.

While I was with the older refugees, a well written newspaper produced by a number of them was finalised and it included an excellent letter, written by a 14 year old, to Ban Ki Moon who was then Head of the United Nations. In it, the young writer appealed for help and pleaded with the UN to ease the pain - mental and physical - being suffered by so many refugees.

When I arrived in Ritsona for the first time, I was pleasantly surprised by the clean conditions - having seen pictures of the Calais Jungle camp in France on the English Channel which is a very different story. When Ritsona was first set up, all refugees lived in tents and living conditions were very bad with extreme heat and mud in the summer and snow and ice in the winter. At Ritsona, all refugees were now living in Iso Box trailers and everyone, including the children, were well dressed and clean with the kids all wearing shoes. The food and clothes were supplied through donations and there were a number of international NGOs involved in the running of the camp - "Echo 100 Plus" from Austria, the aforementioned "I Am You" from Sweden and "Do Your Part" and "Cafe Rits" from the USA - in addition to Light House and CCS. Clothes were distributed by "Echo" on a points system with each individual initially being allocated 150 points per month and each type of clothing being given a certain number of points which were deducted from the 150 as a particular item was handed out. Shoes were in big demand and were worth 60 points. The Iso Box trailers, donated by the United Arab Emirates (UAE), all had electricity, AC, water, heat and bathrooms.

The Camp was initially set up by the Red Crescent and the Greek Red Cross but at some camps, including Ritsona, I was told that corruption had been rampant and that the Greek Army, having been instructed to provide the euro equivalent of $9 of food per person, only gave each refugee $3 to buy food and then pocketed the balance.

On two occasions, we visited another Camp - Oinofyta - which was in a disused chemical factory housing approximately 400 Afghans. This camp was smaller than Ritsona but the Iso Boxes, which also provide accommodation, were positioned inside the old factory building and hence were darker inside than those at Ritsona which sat in the open. Oinofyta did have two small gardens, a library and a school but the trash was worse than that at Ritsona which was surprisingly clean. Morale among the Afghans and the few Pakistanis and Iranians was high and a number of refugees I spoke to were happy with their situation at Oinofyta.

However, one Afghan, with whom I conversed at length, had been an interpreter for the US Army and was distressed that the US Government had reneged on its promise to grant him, as an interpreter, asylum in the USA after his tour of duty with the military and he was now trapped in Greece and was working with the staff at Oinofyta. Sadly there are thousands of Afghans in the same situation who are attempting to flee their country.

At times, it was hard to tell that nearly all inhabitants of Ritsona and Oinofyta were suffering from some form of PTSD after what they had been through in Syria and other countries. Everyone I met and talked to was very polite and courteous although only about 10% spoke English with the main languages being Arabic and Kurdish. I noticed that some Syrian kids often ran off when a Greek Air Force jet flew over from the nearby military airfield - a legacy of the constant pounding they must have had back home from the incessant aerial attacks by so many factions. The continuous circling of US drones in Syria and in other countries, such as Yemen, adds to the likelihood of PTSD - in addition to the slaughter of thousands of innocents through the use of such as the Hellfire drone missile. All the refugees I spoke to were very complimentary about Americans themselves but not at all happy with the US Government and the death and destruction it had caused, along with many other factions, and continues to cause in the Middle East.

The kids were typical kids - not unlike those of the same age in America - but it was obvious a number had pent up anger which they vented by hitting other kids or by trying to steal water bottles, paper, my eyeglasses and even the photos of my grandsons which I took to show them.

At Summer Camp, the kids played soccer, Pass the Parcel, performed gymnastics and participated in a tag game called Shark and in other games that are typically played by small kids around the world. All craft exercises were very popular and even the rowdiest kid would join in and participate with great eagerness sitting on the ground.

The statistics regarding the refugee situation have been quite horrendous. Since 2011, there have been over 11 million Syrian refugees and in 2016 alone there were approximately 365,000 refugees of which 50,000 were now in Greece in approximately 50 detention centers, abandoned buildings and camps. Not long ago, the number of new refugees into Greece dropped to approximately 8,500 with a far larger number arriving in Italy. Whereas the flow of Syrian refugees may have declined into Greece because of restrictions by the Greek government, there are a large number of refugees still endeavoring to get to Europe from such as Afghanistan, Somalia, Libya, Guinea, Nigeria, Bangladesh, Ivory Coast, Gambia, Senegal, Morocco, Mali and the Democratic Republic of the Congo in addition to the majority fleeing the Middle East countries. Italy is now their best landfall after crossing the Mediterranean from Asia and North Africa with some traveling from as far away as Niger and Cameroon. An increasing number of refugees are escaping Yemen where cholera and other diseases such as COVID are killing hundreds on a daily basis. Plus the destruction of that country by Saudi Arabia, with the complicity of the USA, is very distressing. It's reckoned that a child is dying every 10 minutes in Yemen from the consequences of war and disease.

Since early 2015, over 1,000,000 migrants have fled their Middle Eastern and African homes due to war, poverty, drought, persecution etc and a vast number have travelled through Turkey as well as being displaced in their own countries. But the EU and Turkey are now closing the borders and attempts are being made to deport many refugees who are seeking refuge in safer lands. Greece cannot cope financially with the influx of refugees and the uncertainty, which so many refugees feel, is very palpable. A large number of refugees feel forgotten and families are split up and the uncertainty of their future adds to the misery. To make matters worse, Macedonia closed its borders with Greece to refugees and Germany is no longer a safe haven for those looking for a better life. Syria was also one of the countries affected by the immigration ban imposed by the Trump administration - unless Syrian refugees had "bona fide" contacts in the USA. A number of refugees that I spoke to were endeavouring to get to Switzerland, Ireland and even Iceland - all by air where the cost is nearly always prohibitive and the smugglers are not to be trusted.

Upon my return to the USA, by comparison with what the refugees were going through, I had to put up with the minor inconvenience of having my laptop checked into a separate container than my suitcase since I flew home via Istanbul in Turkey - Turkey being one of the six countries where such as laptops were not allowed to be in carry-on baggage on flights to the USA. My arrival experience at JFK - the details of the inconvenience I had to put up with best left for another day - was mind blowing in its inefficiency and suffice it to say that it took two hours from touchdown before I left the airport. This pales into insignificance compared to what so many wonderful people are enduring in refugee camps around Europe.

Whereas the majority of the Syrian refugees blamed President Assad for their woes, they were also critical, not just of the USA, but also of Russia, the UK, Turkey, France and other countries for being complicit in the destruction of their country and their lives and I only hope that I can spread the word that "War is not the Answer". America's foreign policy is adding to the misery of so many innocent people around the world.

My time at Ritsona was a life changing experience and I truly admire the individuals from a number of nations who have devoted their lives to bring peace, security and happiness to the many innocent people who have suffered in so many ways.

By comparison to the stranded refugees, I and the other volunteers had time to enjoy the delights of Chalkida with its good and cheap food and wine. One weekend, a number of my fellow volunteers explored Athens while I discovered Chalkida and its busy waterfront which was lined with many excellent cafes, restaurants and bars. I also hiked up to the ancient castle in the heat and explored the coastline, the lighthouse and a lovely old church. Each morning before heading out to Ritsona, we had a presentation in our hotel on the Greek refugee situation as a whole, a lesson in Arabic, a talk on Islam, a discussion with Medecins sans Frontieres (MSF) on Child Trauma in the Camps and a round table discussion on the advent of what has become known as Voluntourism.

It is hard to describe the anguish and misery that so many refugees have experienced but hopefully my time at Ritsona brought a ray of sunshine - however small - to many whose lives have not been as fortunate as mine. I feel for all of them and sincerely hope the USA will stop aiding in so much destruction in the Middle East and will eventually accept a large number of Syrians and others whose lives have been devastated, in part, by the USA's ceaseless attacks on so many innocents in at least eight countries.

Counterclockwise Clock in La Paz in Bolivia

Deimar on Altiplano in Bolivia

Deimar's family

The Author hiking up Chacaltaya in Bolivia

The Author sand boarding down Cerro Negro in Nicaragua

Graffiti in Nicaragua

Church in El Mozote in El Salvador

The Author in School in San Salvador

Mount Crested Butte Colorado

Ice Bar Crested Butte

The Author in Pirate Costume Contest Crested Butte

# Chapter 16

## Crested Butte, Colorado

---

Mount Crested Butte, at over 12,000 feet, dominates the old mining depot town of Crested Butte which sits at 9,000 feet below the mountain at the top end of the Gunnison Valley in the Colorado Rockies. This iconic mountain does have a crest but, technically, it's not a butte - a butte being a flat topped mesa or table - since its summit is a craggy spiked peak which many hikers, including the author, have staggered to the top.

For 18 years, Lisa, and I owned a property at the base of Mt Crested Butte at Skyland next to The Club at Crested Butte, which has been ranked as one of the top five mountain golf courses in the USA, where I used to play the odd 18 holes. We would spend up to five months a year at Skyland once I had stopped traveling the world as an Aviation Reinsurance Broker but we sold our alpine eden after coming back from our 10 months in France when two of our three children and their families upped sticks and moved from New York City to England - my country of origin which is nearly 5,000 miles from Crested Butte.

Skyland offers staggering views across the valley to the old town of Crested Butte - two miles away - which is surrounded by a further ring of 12,000 foot peaks and is about a mile down valley from the ski resort of Crested Butte which is now owned by Vail Resorts. Not far from Crested Butte are two of the 54 fourteen thousand foot peaks in Colorado.

As a family, we have always been ardent skiers with myself learning to ski in the Austrian and Swiss Alps as a youth and I then transferred that enthusiasm to Lisa and our three kids by initially skiing in New York and Vermont and then going each year for five years to Taos, New Mexico. Our focus then moved on to all the wonderful ski areas in Utah before we decided to try a week at Telluride in southwest Colorado.

Having flown from the East Coast to Denver, we caught the puddle jumper to Montrose which is the gateway airport for Telluride. At this time, we had never heard of Crested Butte so we were intrigued when our flight made a stop in Gunnison and many of the passengers disembarked carrying skis and boots. Our interest peaked when we heard about the delightful old-school ski area called Crested Butte 30 miles up the valley. There and then we decided to check it out the next summer so back we came in June to explore the terrain, albeit without any snow, and to enjoy the hiking which is our second passion.

The land, where the town of Crested Butte now sits, was first occupied by the Ute Native Americans but the discovery of gold in California led to an influx of prospectors who mostly continued moving westwards when it was discovered that there was not a preponderance of gold in the Gunnison Valley. However, it was soon learned that coal was in abundance in the mountains and many miners from Central Europe found their way to this spectacular valley which sits about 250 miles southwest of Denver.

Crested Butte - or CB as it's known - was incorporated as a mining depot town in 1880 with a small population of miners and prospectors from as far away as Croatia, Serbia, Italy, England, Scotland and other European countries which had a history of mining. Many of these families are still in the Valley today having turned to ranching and skiing once the last mine closed in 1952 and a ski area opened up in the early 60s. As the saying goes, CB moved from "Black Gold to White Gold" as CB slowly became one of the most attractive unspoiled ski areas in the USA.

In winter, there is only one way in and one way out of CB - from Gunnison - so, with just the one escape route, crime is at a minimum for most of the year. In summer, two unpaved passes to the west and east - Kebler and Cottonwood Passes - are open but they are closed from early November to normally around the beginning of June. The disused mines are still up in the mountains and the mind boggles at how the coal was brought down to CB by mule and mountain railroad for onward transportation to the refineries further east and south. CB's strategic position at the head of the valley led it to becoming a very important mining depot town for approximately 70 years.

The old town of CB has been superbly preserved with no traffic lights, a 15 mph speed limit, no fire sirens, no neon, fluorescent or LED signs and even the new buildings on Elk Avenue (Main Street) look as if they were built in 1880. There is a very different culture in CB than in most communities in the USA with the majority of houses and cars left unlocked (unless black bears have been reported in town) and there is an official hitchhiking station on the edge of town with a sign put up by the Township asking drivers to pull off the road to pick up riders. The majority of the riders are looking to go 30 miles down valley to Gunnison where Western State Colorado University (WSCU) sits but a number of riders are also hoping to get to Denver to the northeast or to the likes of Grand Junction to the west.

I picked up many riders over the years - as did Lisa. In fact, she once picked up three different riders at three different spots on her way to Gunnison and I once picked up a delightful fellow about 10 miles west of Gunnison who admitted that he'd just broken out of a rehab center to the south of Gunnison and was now attempting to reunite with his family in Montrose. And I too have hitchhiked many times up and down the Gunnison Valley. A well known clever system of hand singles tells the driver how far the rider wishes to go.

When we first came to CB in the summer, we decided on our second day to hike to Aspen which is about 12 miles to the north but the hike requires a climb over West Maroon Pass at 12,500 feet and then a long hike down the valley past the mountains known as the Maroon Bells and on into Aspen. Aspen was one of the first skiing towns in the Rockies and CB looks like Aspen probably did 50 years ago. We immediately fell in love with the mountains and the beautiful wild flowers that blanket the valley in June and July. The fall colours are to be seen to be believed with the yellow and orange aspens and cottonwoods mingling with the evergreens - all this beauty sitting below the snow capped peaks. We soon realised that CB was our sort of town - especially since the only police car we saw was an all wheel Outback with two mountain bikes strapped to the trunk. It looked to us that CB had got its priorities right.

For a number of years, I worked in Guest Services at the ski area which mostly involved leading ski tours around the mountain and assisting the excellent Ski Patrol by being in radio contact with the Patrol's base and reporting and assisting with the many accidents on the mountain. It was always a long, but rewarding, day which involved two early briefings - one at base and another at the Ski Patrol hut close to the top of the mountain. CB is a challenging mountain with a third of the ski area being deemed as Extreme but there is plenty of Intermediate and Advanced terrain for skiers of all levels and I enjoyed showing visitors that there was nothing to be afraid of. I also led snowshoe tours where guests rode a lift up the mountain, donned their snowshoes and then hiked back down the mountain, often in deep snow, to the Base area.

I also volunteered with the Adaptive Sports program, for those who are physically and mentally challenged, during winter and summer. In winter, I skied with a variety of wonderful individuals - from kids with Aspergers, Autism and Down Syndrome to blind skiers and many war veterans who sadly had lost limbs in one of our many worldwide conflicts. And a number of the veterans were suffering from PTSD with one or two, perhaps having been blown up in a crowded Middle East bazaar, being terrified of other people so finding a ski slope for them which was empty of other skiers was always a challenge. The special equipment used is nearly all made in France and, when living in southwest France not long ago, we came across the same four wheeled summer equipment which was bringing clients down the mountain which sits above the pilgrimage town of Lourdes.

The Adaptive summer program offered the same clients canoeing, rock climbing, mountain biking and horseback riding. One day, I was at a ranch holding the reins of rather testy nag called John Wayne in order to allow a large limbless ex Marine to be hoisted into the saddle when John Wayne decided he'd had enough and bit me on my right shoulder - luckily without inflicting any permanent damage. Afterwards, I delighted in telling folks that I had been bitten by John Wayne. This produced amusing comments such as "I thought John Wayne was dead" or "Was he drunk"! It turned out that the equine JW was having a bad day and was suffering from worms.

Another surprising event in CB was the time our garage floor collapsed causing our two Outbacks to fall into a deep pit. We had just arrived from the East Coast one January and a lot of snow had fallen during the preceding weeks. Hearing a bang in the night, we assumed it was snow falling off the roof but, much to my surprise, on opening the side door to the garage, there were our two cars lying in what had been the bottom of our empty undeveloped basement over which the garage had been built.

The house had been constructed over 30 years earlier and the wooden tresses that supported the basement floor had rotted out and the weight of the two cars was too much to bear. Many of our friends came to watch the cars being extracted with the older of the two being deemed a total loss by the Insurance Adjuster who had arrived on the scene very soon after the catastrophe. After the older car was towed away to the dump, the newer of the two cars needed $7,000 of repairs which the Insurer paid without hesitation and he then paid us a princely sum for the older of the two cars.

Outbacks are worth a lot more in the Rockies than they are in New Jersey so I flew back east and found a similar model of the same age with about 20,000 fewer miles at a Honda dealer for a price which was considerably less than the Insurer had paid us for the destroyed car. The shock to the system on seeing the two cars in a 10 foot hole cannot be described.

Apart from the wonderful skiing and hiking, CB has superb fly fishing for trout and a fresh water salmon known by its Native American name of Kokanee. We had a number of fun family fishing days on the Gunnison and East Rivers with our daughters who lived on the East Coast and our son who attended WSCU. He managed to graduate in just over 4 years which was quite unusual considering the many distractions such as mountain biking, skiing, hiking, climbing, kayaking, white water rafting and fly fishing.

We took a guide one day with us on a family fishing outing on a stretch of river we weren't familiar with and, when I claimed the first prize, having caught 18 trout, I was promptly disqualified as I had also caught a bush and the guide's baseball cap.

CB is never at a loss for a party or a competition and the most challenging ski race, where I would act as a volunteer, is the Grand Traverse where pairs depart the Base of the ski area at midnight, equipped with headlamps, and climb the mountains to the north of CB and then ski down to Aspen. Time and fitness checks are made at various points along the way at old 10th Mountain Division huts and any skier who separates from his or her partner is disqualified - as is anyone who does not meet the physical and time criterias. My job was to drive those disqualified back to base from the highest position along the route that I could get to in my Outback and many of those in my car were not happy to have been thrown off this challenging event having trained for weeks. The winner normally arrived in Aspen after close to eight hours of climbing and skiing and approximately 7,000 feet of aggregate vertical.

Another fun ski race is the annual Al Jolson in honour of the mailman who delivered mail on skis to Aspen in the late 1800s. Apart from the few who were determined to win this climbing and skiing race, many racers skied in costume either singly or as groups - including a group of four "salmon" who, having skied a section downhill, would then ski back uphill in true salmon fashion - akin to what salmon do as they head upstream and over waterfalls.

There are annual Music and Arts Festivals in CB and there's never a shortage of music groups playing at bars and at the base area. Our favorite wine bar, The Princess, named after the old movie theater that used to be on its site, had an old friend of ours from West Virginia playing his country folk there and another favorite singer was the head of the Ski Patrol. There are also snowmobile towed ski jump races down Elk Avenue and there used to be the tradition of "naked skiing" down Mount Crested Butte on the last day of each ski season which sadly has now been stopped. And the over 30 restaurants and bars in CB provide an excellent variety of international food of all kinds.

There is also a superb Crested Butte Film Festival in the fall - which I was asked to help publicise - and it now rivals the far better known Sundance Festival. There is also a wonderful pagan festival from Eastern Europe called Vinotok which culminates in everyone "throwing" their bad karma into a bonfire at the bottom of Elk Avenue. Unfortunately, the surfeit of "spirits" results in items other than karma being disposed of in the bonfire - items such as laptops, IPhones and other pieces of electrical equipment.

An event held at the Ice Bar at about 10,000 feet at the ski area, which I was proud to win once and to come in second twice, was the Pirate Costume Contest sponsored by Gosling's Rum from Bermuda. A Dark and Stormy (Gosling's Dark Rum and Ginger Beer) was the favorite cocktail at around 3pm each day at the Ice Bar to be consumed before skiing back down to Base when the lifts closed at 4 pm. Pirates drink a lot of rum - hence the need for a Pirate Costume Contest - and my outfit of tricorn hat, white blouse, long black jacket and black boots with my stuffed parrot named "Notlob" sitting on my shoulder - see Monty Python's Dead Parrot sketch - was always sufficient to catch the judge's eye.

CB has an excellent Museum where I was a Docent and from where the Curator led intriguing historical walking tours - sometimes involving a fun pub crawl where, apart from drinking the odd ale, each venue visited had a character from CB's past.

Over a 20 year period, Lisa and I experienced the very special flavor of one of the most fascinating communities in the USA. There is no side to anyone who lives there - money, class, race are all meaningless - and everyone treats and helps each other with the utmost respect and decency and there's never a shortage of kindly souls to help those in distress.

It was with some sadness that we decided to sell our home away from home after 20 years out west but, with two thirds of our family across the Atlantic in Europe, our focus was eastwards instead of west. Our love for France and the Peak District in northern England means we are spending a lot of each year in La Belle France and Blighty. This also includes time with our extended family and grandsons in Cheshire and Surrey in addition to exploring, hiking and loving village life in both England and France. Southwest France, close to Spain and the Pyrenees, is near and dear to us but, in the not too distant future, we hope to venture west again to enjoy the pleasures of life at 9,000 feet.

# Chapter 17

## Coast to Coast – A Walk across England

In 1972, an Englishman, Alfred Wainwright, carried out the first recorded walk across the North of England from Coast to Coast. His route started at St Bees Head on the Irish Sea and took him up and over the hills of the Lake District and across the Yorkshire Dales, the Vale of York and the North Yorkshire Moors - ending up at the small fishing village of Robin Hood's Bay on the North Sea.

Walking from West to East meant that he had the strong westerly winds off the Atlantic and Irish Sea at his back and that the often frequent rains would not be in his face. Since then this approximately 200 mile walk has become a rite of passage for many walkers from around the world.

A few years ago, Lisa and I decided to follow in Alfred Wainwright's footsteps and we signed up with the Sierra Club for this two week trek. We chose the Sierra Club because we have been ardent supporters of this environmental club for many years - a club which was founded by John Muir in 1892 to initially preserve Yellowstone and Sequoia National Parks in California's natural beauty. Preservation of our National Parks is even more important in today's technical age where the political power of the oil, gas and fracking industries is doing so much harm to the beauty and future of the environment.

There are many English based walking companies that we could have chosen from but our support for the Sierra Club was paramount to us - plus we knew we would be joined on a number of days by locals with their deep knowledge of the geography and history of the route that we would be following.

We initially stayed with friends on the edge of the Lake District near the town of Kendal and did a couple of testing walks over the hills and dales to get us into shape. We then joined the other seven walkers - plus a guide and his tail end charlie cohort - in the town of Carlisle from where we were transported to our starting point in St Bees on the Irish Sea.

Our driver for the entire two week slog was a delightful local called John Lightfoot who soon became known to us all as Twinkle Toes. Twinkle Toes' job was to haul our overnight gear each day from bed and breakfast, or pub, where we had been staying, to the next one. This allowed us to hike the average distance of 12 miles per day with only a light day pack for water and snacks. Thankfully, there was no camping along the way and we always ended up each evening with a hot shower, a delicious supper and the odd local beer in some delightful hostelry – often in the middle of nowhere.

The composition of our group was made up of a charming Park Ranger from Yellowstone National Park, an Indian lady who was on the faculty at the University of Minnesota and a retired High School principal and his wife from California. Plus a mother and her son who appeared to be doing this hike as some form of therapy for the son for an issue which was not obvious to us. The seventh individual, a Texan, did not last even the first day of walking as it was obvious to all that he was totally incapable of any serious activity - a fact that was immediately made obvious to us on the first evening when he struggled to walk up the hill to supper in a restaurant in St Bees. It was politely suggested to him on day one that it would be better for him to fly back home - or he could ride with Twinkle Toes and join us at our accommodation at the end of each day. He chose the latter.

We have remained good friends with the Indian lady (a Parsee) and have subsequently hiked with her in Colorado and Minnesota. The school principal's wife was an expert on wild flora around the world, including the United Kingdom, and she added a fascinating addition to our group with her knowledge of all the English wild flowers and shrubs.

Our leader from California was quite charming but sadly he was a hopeless navigator and on a number of occasions he had to be advised as to the correct heading to take - even though this was the third time he'd walked the Coast to Coast. He had a GPS/SatNav which thankfully did not work as all the fun of a long walk of this nature is in self-navigation by the various landmarks and the use of a good old fashioned compass and a map.

We set out from St Bees with the traditional wetting of our hiking boots in the Irish Sea – as Wainwright had done - and our first steep pitch came straight away when we hiked up the cliffs which surround St Bees to flatter land at the top. We then headed east to Cleator Moor following our maps and our compass - heading towards the testing but spectacular Lake District which would prove to be the toughest section of our walk. We were joined by a couple of locals on the first day and for the next three days we were led by the wonderful Derek who has become a firm friend of ours. He has stayed and hiked with us in Colorado and will hopefully be coming to see us in the village of Tideswell in the Derbyshire Peak District when we are there in the future.

Derek has a wonderful north country Cumbrian accent and, after hiking in the mountains around Crested Butte in Colorado with a local friend, our friend put in a request to Derek after chatting with him for twenty minutes as we sipped beers at the end of a long and strenuous day - "Derek" - he said - "would you please mind speaking in English".

Derek lives on the Irish Sea to the north of St Bees in the town of Whitehaven and, now in his 70s, he's worked since the age of 16 in the same nuclear waste clean up factory in nearby Sellafield. He has also run a Lake District Mountain Rescue Team for many years and one evening on our Coast to Coast hike he gave us all a fascinating talk on the many rescues his team had carried out. One thing he stressed was that many accidents occur in the last couple of hours of the day when walkers are tired, and perhaps overconfident, and shortcuts are mistakenly taken. And a lack of map reading skills and how to interpret the scale means that many walkers take on distances which are far greater than they had intended to walk.

We trekked on up into the Lake District where we experienced the only wet day of our two week adventure. But, boy, did it rain. The water poured down the mountain which we were hiking up and even our foul weather gear proved to be useless. We spoke little as we hauled ourselves up with the water gushing down on top of us. It was the only day that we were rained upon which is highly unusual on this higher ground which is subject to the wet westerly winds which flow from off the Atlantic and then hit the rugged Lake District terrain.

After passing through Ennerdale with its isolated Black Sail Youth Hostel hut, we reached the delightful village of Grasmere - home to the poet William Wordsworth. We didn't know it at the time but we later learned that we were staying in a Quaker retreat which masqueraded as a small hotel. Those of my readers who enjoyed the TV series Fawlty Towers will remember the two little old ladies who would come down the stairs together holding hands and greet Basil Fawlty with a "Good Morning Mr Fawlty". Lo and behold, on our first morning, two little old ladies came down the stairs of our accommodation, holding hands, and greeted Lisa with "Good Morning - are you having a nice walk".

It turned out that our fellow walkers were all Fawlty Towers fanatics and so there were many jokes about Fawlty Towers during the rest of the walk. Such as the many rude comments that Basil made to guests and to Manuel his Spanish waiter. And to cap it all, when Lisa and I were on the platform at York railway station after our two week adventure - waiting to catch a train to London after staying with my Australian cousin who lived nearby - who should come striding down the platform than none other than John Cleese who played Basil in the series. Some may remember his Silly Walk from Monty Python and this time he was striding along - not realising that the whole world was pointing at him - doing a slightly more relaxed version of his Silly Walk.

After Grasmere, we headed further into the Lake District and stayed the night in Glenridding on Ullswater. Interestingly, only one lake is actually called a Lake in the Lake District with most of them known as "Water". From there, we struggled onwards to Shap with its fine Abbey and we then cheated a bit - as we also did a second time. We got Twinkle Toes to transport us across the flat countryside to the old town of Kirkby Stephen on the edge of the Yorkshire Dales. Kirkby means "Settlement by a Church" in old English - the church supposedly named after St Stephen - while Kirk is also a Norse/Scottish word for a church.

From Kirkby Stephen, we hiked up onto the staggeringly beautiful Yorkshire Dales where we stopped for a picnic lunch at Nine Standards Rigg. Nine Standards Rigg is a collection of nine large stone cairns standing on the moors at an elevation of over 2,000 feet. A cairn is a vertical pile of dry stones with the smaller ones on the top and the origin of these particular cairns is unknown but they must have been there for over 1,000 years.

From there, we ploughed on across the rather soggy moor, with no signs to show the way, with map and compass in hand. Wainwright was insistent that no blazes or sign posts should guide walkers along the Coast to Coast so that all participants could plot their own route across the country - nearly always from West to East. A few hardy souls sometimes trek from East to West - with the wind in their faces - from the North Sea to the Irish Sea after accomplishing the hike going the other way.

The Norse and the Danes, who were the principal raiders of the English east coast, got as far south as East Anglia and almost to London. They also occupied Scotland and the North of England and the counties of Cumbria and Yorkshire through which the Coast to Coast runs. Many places have names from the Old Norse - including the river Swale which runs through Swaledale where we hiked in the Yorkshire Dales.

After struggling across the moors on our way to little Keld, we came across a wonderful Norse family who owned the lovely Raven Farm. With a daughter named Raven and an offer of cream teas, it was a must to stop there to catch our breath, eat the delicious scones washed down with home brewed tea while we listened to the skylarks' and curlews' birdsong as they hovered over the adjacent farmland.

It was in Keld that we met up with John who was born and bred and still lived in the ancient town of Richmond but surprisingly had worked for a number of years at the Cummins Diesel plant in Columbus Indiana. John was a fount of local lore and we walked with him along the river Swale to Richmond where we took our first day off from trudging across the country. John was amazed that I could still spout the names of the Yorkshire rivers that flow into the North Sea - the Swale, the Ure, the Nidd, the Wharf, the Aire, the Calder and the Don. It's extraordinary that something I learned in school at the age of eight is still lodged in my feeble brain.

Luckily, John knew the lady who was the ex-Mayor of Richmond and she gave us an intriguing tour of the town and castle and that evening we all repaired to a local pub where John played the accordion in the pub's band. Needless to say, many ales were consumed that night – as were quaffed on many other nights along the way. The favourite beer proved to be the creamy Theakston ale followed by Black Sheep - so named as the heir apparent to the Theakston brewery had fallen out with his father and formed his own brewery having become the black sheep of the family. Most beers in the North of England are pulled by lever from the basement with no carbonation as there is in the majority of beers in the USA. This means the head is deliciously creamy and the taste delightfully smooth.

At Richmond, early the next morning, I walked around the ancient abandoned turf racecourse on the moor above the town which is still used by local trainers for early morning workouts for their nags. It was soon time to move on eastwards and we cheated again. We got dear old Twinkle Toes to drive us across the flat Vale of York and up onto the barren North Yorkshire Moors for two more days of walking - with one night in an old farmhouse where we were entertained by the farmer and his son. I knew the Vale of York of old as I had achieved my Royal Navy flying wings at an RAF station in the Vale.

It was then on to our final destination - Robin Hood's Bay - where we dipped our boots in the North Sea in honour of Wainwright who did the same on completion of his long walk many years ago. Robin Hood's Bay is near the town of Whitby where we spent our final night. Whitby is famous for its Abbey, which we explored, and it was also the location for Bram Stoker's "Dracula" which he wrote in 1897.

It was time to bid farewell to our new found friends after a scintillating two weeks – with never an angry word or silly argument with folks we'd never met before. There was just the occasional nudge to get our leader heading in the right direction. After all, his wife, who had been with us that first day in Carlisle, had told us, before we headed out, that her husband always got lost. Not very reassuring at the start of a 200 mile marathon on paths unknown. He also always insisted that we went for supper in one of the many pubs at 6 pm. This meant a surfeit of pre-supper ales as the majority of English pubs up North do not serve supper until 7.30 pm at the earliest - and woe betide anyone who attempts to take their leftovers from a meal back to their accommodation. This is an absolute No No in England and is rightfully respected. All in all a wonderful experience which convinced us to subsequently walk around the island of Orkney and much of the northwest of Scotland which we did at a later date.

# Chapter 18

## Skiing in the Chilean Andes

---

Chile is a slender country running from the driest desert in the world, Atacama, in the north down towards Antarctica with its ice and snow at the bottom of South America. The country lies to the south of Peru and to the west of Bolivia and Argentina. The Andes mountains, the same chain as the Rockies, start in northwestern Canada and run south through the western USA, Central America and South America and cover one third of western Chile - alongside the Pacific Ocean.

The tallest peak in Chile is Aconcagua, the highest mountain in both the southern and western hemispheres, which sits at 22,841 feet. And Punta Arenas - close to Cape Horn and Antarctica - is the southernmost city in the world - a city technically having to have a cathedral.

Chile is approximately 2,700 miles long but, on average, only 110 miles wide and it enjoys a wide variety of climates due to its north/south orientation. It has many volcanoes running down its spine and a number of these volcanoes are still active and many thermal hot springs (agua termales in Spanish) dot the landscape on higher ground - some of them sitting on a number of ski areas.

The capital of Chile is Santiago which sits in a bowl between the Andes and the Pacific at a height which varies between 1,600 feet and 2,100 feet. With a population of around 6.5M, there is a high pollution level in the city since the westerly air off the Pacific is trapped by the surrounding Andes.

Chile was occupied by Spain in 1520 and didn't gain its independence until 1823. A subsequent major conflict called the War of the Pacific in 1879 was fought with Peru and Bolivia over the territorial rights to the minerals in the Atacama desert. A military coup, with the support of the USA, took place on September 11 1973 when the democratically elected President - Salvador Allende - committed suicide and right wing General Augusto Pinochet took control of the country for the next 25 years. Many people were arrested, tortured and killed under the military regime until Pinochet was arrested on a trip to Great Britain in 1998. He was sent back to Chile in 2000 for medical reasons and remained there under house arrest, awaiting trial on hundreds of charges, until his death in 2006.

The ski season in Chile - as it is elsewhere in the southern hemisphere - is during the northern summer and I've skied there four times with a number of my family. My first trip south was with our second daughter and our son and we flew to Santiago on Lan Chile via Miami. Arriving in the early morning, we took a van to Valle Nevado (Valley of Snow in Spanish) which sits a short distance from Santiago with its base at around 10,000 feet. Arriving at our hotel to find that we could not check in until 5 pm, we decided to ski all day and then had the most delicious steak dinner imaginable. Going rapidly to sleep that night, all three of us woke up the next morning with altitude sickness having gone from the Santiago airport at around 1,500 feet to 10,000 feet in a very short time. The cure was to ski all day and drink copious amounts of water and all was well thereafter. Other ski areas close to Valle Nevado - all connected - are La Parva, El Colorado and Farellones and one amazing run is from the top of Valle Nevado at around 12,000 feet down to the valley floor where a taxi is required to get skiers back to the base at Valle Nevado.

We next spent three nights in Santiago staying in the Hotel Carrera in a room from which a bazooka had been fired in 1973 in an attempt to kill President Allende who was in the nearby Palacio de la Moneda, the Presidential Palace. Our stay in Santiago involved riding the amazingly clean, efficient and timely subway, visiting the zoo and attending a Chilean professional premier league football (soccer) match between Universidad de Chile and Cobreloa, a team from a city in the Atacama desert called Calama.

From Santiago, we took a car to the lovely Hotel Portillo which sits high up in the Andes close to the Argentinian border at around 9,000 feet. The hotel, completed in 1942, sits in isolation with its own beautiful ski area in the shadow of Mt Aconcagua, The service in the hotel was superb with the same three red coated gentlemen waiting on us hand and foot at our table each day and all the cosmopolitan skiers met in the bar for cocktails before dinner each evening. It was there that we met the Argentinians, Veronica and Marcelo, from Buenos Aires who subsequently invited us to stay with them and ski at Las Lenas in the Argentinian Andes on a subsequent trip down south.

Portillo has four of the only ski lifts in the world which cannot be destroyed by avalanches since there are no pylons to carry gondolas or chair lifts. Instead, five skiers are towed abreast on their skis up the steep mountain on a triangular system known as "Va et Vient" - or "Go and Come" in French.

One day we went heli skiing in an ancient French Alouette helicopter with a broken altimeter. This involved flying to around 15,000 feet close to Aconcagua and then skiing for most of the day to get back down to the Hotel Portillo. The hotel sits on the shores of the Laguna del Inca and a number of ski runs end up at the shore of the lake. If the lake is frozen, skiers ski back to the hotel on the ice. If the lake is not frozen, a boat is sent from the hotel to pick up the skiers.

The only other occupants of this high altitude terrain close to the hotel were soldiers in the Chilean Army who were based in a small encampment in order to learn the rudiments of alpine skiing and fighting.

After Portillo, we headed to Termas de Chillan - another ski area which is about six hours south of Santiago down the Pan American Highway. At Termas, our hotel's swimming pool was always bubbling with warm thermal water and the skiing was totally unlimited. One day we hired a Chilean guide for some backcountry skiing beneath the two volcanoes which dominate Termas and were surprised to learn that our guide had been taught to ski in Vernon Valley New Jersey. Termas ski area is now known as Nevados de Chillan - meaning "Snows of Chillan" which replaced "Thermal Hot Springs of Chillan" in English.

Another trip to Chile to ski with my son saw us again at Termas de Chillan and was followed by a five hour drive further south to the lovely town of Pucon. Pucon sits on a gorgeous lake and is dominated by the volcano named Villarica where we safely skied although it did erupt more recently with many houses in Pucon being destroyed. We had originally flown to Buenos Aires to ski at Las Lenas but a lack of snow forced us to head over to Santiago after a wonderful stay with Veronica and Marcello which included yet another fun football match - this time between Boca Juniors and Argentina Juniors in the Argentinian top league.

Before leaving Termas for Pucon, my son and I were involved that morning in a minor avalanche which occurred inbounds - luckily with no injuries to us. On checking into our hotel in Pucon, we were asked where we had come from and, on saying Termas, we were told that two skiers were missing at Termas. We subsequently learned that two snowboarders had been killed in an avalanche at Termas in the backcountry not far from where we had experienced our own slide. I've always been told that the way to avoid avalanches is to never ski on a slope greater than 30 degrees pitch but that is not much fun for a decent skier.

On another trip to ski in Chile, I headed south by train from Santiago and stayed at the Mission Impossible (M.I.) Lodge in Las Trancas close to the Termas de Chillan ski area. M.I. Lodge was owned by a French couple - Bertrand and Maylis - and was the ultimate "party central". A great team of international youngsters worked there - mainly from Chile, France, Argentina, Peru and Brazil including one young Frenchman - Sebastian - known to all as Sea Bass. Sea Bass came from St Jean de Luz near Biarritz in southwest France - close to Salies de Bearn the old town where we have twice lived for long periods and is the town which experienced a massive flood causing us to head back to the USA earlier than intended not long ago. Sea Bass had an amazing northern English accent from Blackpool in Lancashire and, on first meeting him, we assumed he was English but he had never been to England having learned his English from a Blackpudlian friend who too had a strong Lancashire accent. I subsequently went back again to M. I. Lodge with son, Rich, and his wife Camille - pronounced, as in the French, Camee.

The original third partner in the M.I. Lodge was another Frenchman - Jerome - who sold up and surprisingly moved to Crested Butte Colorado - our home for 18 years - where he became a good friend. One evening at M.I. Lodge, the owners closed up the shop and invited all the clients and staff to a disco in the village of Las Trancas for a night of frivolity and far too much alcohol.

On another occasion, I again travelled by train from Santiago to Chillan and on to Termas - returning at the end of my stay by bus back to Santiago.

The service on both train and bus was quite superb with the bus providing menus and a full meal. Two waiters on the bus radioed the food orders ahead in advance and, when the bus later stopped along the way, the waiters picked up the meals and served them to the passengers on trays with small white tablecloths. And the bus provided blankets and cushions and ran excellent movies on the TVs.

On my long drives from Santiago southwards, I was stopped a number of times for speeding on the Pan American Highway by Chilean carabineros (police) but I always carried with me a New York City policeman's ID card - a gift from my secretary who was married to a city cop. Producing this always worked a treat. Speeding fines had to be paid on the spot with non-payers being carted off to jail until the money was produced but luckily my fake police card always resulted in no fine - just a friendly warning - and I was able to avoid the night in a less than attractive police cell.

Flying to and from the USA to Chile on the various South American airlines such as Lan Chile and Avianca etc was always a delightful experience although I was stuck for the night on one trip in a hotel in Miami (at the airline's expense) when the aircraft experienced mechanical problems.

The most unpleasant flying experience I had during my four trips to Chile was with security at Denver airport on my way to Santiago. On going through security, I was required to have my hands and back pack swabbed and was then told that I had explosive material on my hands. I was whisked off to a private room for a full body search and when asked when I had last handled explosive materials, I delighted in telling the agents that it was many moons ago when I had been the Ordnance Officer in an F4 squadron at NAS Miramar in San Diego where I had handled such as napalm and 500 lb bombs. At that, security let me go without explaining what it was all about - and, of course, they told me to have a "Good Flight".

As can be seen, Chile is a fascinating country with lovely people, excellent food and staggeringly varied scenery and a terrain which is a dream for all outdoor lovers. Not just because of the superb skiing but also the fly fishing, mountaineering, kayaking and canoeing.

# Chapter 19

## Salies de Bearn – La Vie en France

---

Salies de Bearn is an idyllic medieval village of around 5,000 residents in the Department of Pyrenees - Atlantiques in southwest France not far from Spain, the Pyrenees mountains and the three French Basque provinces.

Or it was idyllic until the night of June 12/13 2018 when the Saleys river in the heart of the town rose approximately 50 feet, came over the top and flooded the town to a depth of over five feet. About 65% of the town was wiped out, including the majority of the shops, businesses and restaurants and all ground floor residents (mostly older folk) had to be evacuated before the water had receded about 18 hours later.

There had been much rain all spring and in early June and, combined with the snow melt from the Pyrenees, all the rivers in the province of Bearn des Gaves, where Salies sits, had been very swollen and it only needed torrential rain for two days prior to the flood to put the level over the top - as it did in other towns in the area although none of them were devastated to the same degree as Salies.

Lisa and I had been living in a rented house, built in 1628, for six weeks when the "inondation" (flood) hit us and we were trapped upstairs all night and most of the next day until the water subsided leaving about three inches of mud on the ground floor. The water level in our house reached around three feet and our fridge and kitchen table and chairs floated as the water was moving through the house at considerable speed.

With the old narrow streets and alleyways, the speed of the water rushing through Salies sometimes reached around 30 mph so our rental car, and many other cars, didn't stand a chance of survival with a number of them being washed away or into other cars. In fact, our car had water in it up to the dashboard and was full of mud after the water had subsided.

Luckily, nobody in Salies was killed, nor hurt, and the "pompiers" (firemen) and the "gendarmes" (police) did an excellent job of rescuing residents by boat and dinghy but the majority of the kitchens in the houses were destroyed and two of our friends, who owned restaurants, felt that they would never be able to open up their businesses again.

Our house had three floors and we were able to move our belongings to a higher level so all our possessions and clothes remained intact. We had our daughter and her two sons (13 and 10) from New York City staying with us and the boys were magnificent - spending most of the next day mopping up the mud and helping move the ruined sofas and chairs out onto the street.

Our house was now uninhabitable so we decided to leave France and return to Cranbury New Jersey two weeks earlier than we had originally planned. It would have been a two month stay in this lovely town where we had lived for ten months in 2015/16. A kind friend offered us a bed in his old farmhouse but his elderly wife had Alzheimer's and, with no car, we didn't feel it appropriate to impose ourselves upon them. Instead, we booked a room for two nights in the old Hotel du Parc in town, took a lengthy taxi ride to Bordeaux, stayed the night in a hotel at the airport, bought expensive one way flights back to the USA and arrived back at our house in Cranbury - none the worse for wear having experienced an event of a lifetime which shattered so many of our French friends' lives. Amusingly, our French taxi driver to Bordeaux was a young girl named Cyndi since her mother adored Cyndi Lauper.

The cost of abandoning Salies and getting back to the USA was not inconsiderable but we felt so sorry for our many French friends and we subsequently had pangs of remorse about leaving France and not sticking around to help with the clean up. But with no car and nowhere to live, in hindsight, we felt we had made the right decision.

Our travel insurance only covered Trip Interruption for a Natural Disaster if it involved our Primary Residence, which was obviously not in Salies, and a fight took place with our rental car company, Europcar, regarding the cost of repairs to the damage caused by the flood. Europcar initially tried to charge us $14,000 for the car but we eventually won the battle as our credit card's insurance paid the final net charge after we had fought with Europcar for many months over the cost of the damage to the car which obviously we had no control over. Not only was the car inoperable but Europcar also tried to charge us around $2,000 for fuel and towing costs after the gendarmes had ordered all cars to be towed away so the mud, which covered the streets, could be cleaned up when the town slowly came back to life. It was a sad end to our second stay in a town which we love so much.

We have many charming French friends in and around Salies and, not long before the Flood, we had held a "Soiree de Retour" (Coming Back Party) for 20 folks as a follow up to the "Soiree d'Adieu" (Goodbye Party) we had held two years earlier.

This "Inondation" was a one in fifty year event - hopefully never to occur again - and Salies de Bearn at the best of times demonstrates all the wonderful qualities that life in southwest France has to offer. Founded over 600 years ago on the river Saleys, it wasn't until the Middle Ages that it was discovered that this delightful "village" (as all towns in the region of Bearn are called if the population is less than 7,000) was sitting on salt beds - salt being a major commodity in those days. Two "chasseurs" (hunters) had shot and wounded a "sanglier" (a wild boar) which they came across much later lying dead - encrusted in salt. Realising the village was situated on a major commodity, a new industry sprang up which led to the building of Les Thermes (a salt spa) in Victorian times which is there to this day. The spa in turn led to the building of the Hotel du Parc to accommodate the many visitors from as far away as Paris who came, and still do come, to enjoy the salt baths. Household salt is still an important product in Salies and an annual "Fete du Sel" (Festival of Salt) is held each fall which brings in around 10,000 people - many dressed in their traditional regional costumes - to enjoy the food, wine and dancing in recognition of the historic importance of salt. The 'Musee de Sel' (Museum of Salt), where the town's history with salt is well presented, is certainly worth a visit.

The French believe in "Working to Live" which is a little different from the crazy American lifestyle of "Living to Work" and it takes some getting used to the fact that most businesses and shops are closed for two hours at lunchtime - a meal which is enjoyed by all the family, including the children, who have a break from school to eat with their parents and often their grandparents too. Amazingly, a doctor I saw made house calls every morning from 9 am to noon, went home for lunch with his family from noon to 2 pm and then saw patients in his office from 2 pm to 11 pm at night. And he personally answered the phone and told me to come along at 9:15 pm on the night when I had called to make an appointment.

Restaurants closing after lunch at 2.30 pm and not reopening for supper until 7.30 pm or 8.00 pm requires getting used to and many rural restaurants are owned and run by extended families with granny being the "Meeter and Greeter", the husband and his wife the chefs and the kids/grandkids the wait staff. This is done for reduced family tax reasons and it means that many restaurants offer a delightful ambience with no incentive to eat up and leave - as described later in this chapter..

Three French words aptly describe life in rural France - Tranquille, Agreable and Enchantee.

The first two words are self obvious about the peaceful and agreeable lifestyle and people and the third word - Enchantee - used when meeting someone for the first time, is, to me, far more attractive than our rather mundane "Pleased to Meet You". All pedestrians greet passers by with a cordial "bonjour", total strangers shake hands with everyone in a bar or cafe and fellow diners offer a "bon appetit" to other diners as they pass by their table on the way to their own. And an "Enchantee" often involves two or three side kisses on the cheek - known as "bises".

Although French is the primary language, Bearnais is also spoken by some of the older residents in the province of Bearn and the word Salies means saline (as in salt) in Bearnais and the aforementioned Gave is the Bearnais word for a river. Salies sits about 40 minutes from the historic town of Biarritz which is on the Atlantic and close to Bayonne (pronounced "Bye-yonne" not "Bay-yone") which is where the bayonet was invented and is also famous for its ham and chocolate.

The old town of Pau, birthplace of Henri IV (1553-1610), is 40 minutes to the east and the Spanish border is close by with the magnificent town of San Sebastian about 70 minutes away. The Basque "Pintxos" (Tapas) in the Old Town of San Sebastian are not to be missed.

The French Basque provinces in the foothills of the Pyrenees have many delightful villages - not least Espelette which holds an intriguing market every Wednesday where shaggy work horses are often auctioned off - horses that are used to pull large tree trunks out of forests since mechanised equipment is unable to do so. Salies also has a Thursday market which is the social event of the week and the fish sold there, which comes from St Jean de Luz on the Atlantic, is a must for supper every Market Day.

Being very keen hikers, Lisa and I covered over 400 miles during our time in Salies - locally in Bearn but also on the GR 10 trail which runs along the Pyrenees between the Atlantic and the Mediterranean. The "Grand Randonnee Dix" (GR 10) is a spectacular trail with magnificent vistas connecting delightful mountain villages - each with its auberge (inn), gite (cottage) or chambres d'hote (B & B) as places to stay. "Grand Randonnee" translates as Big Hike in English. Many of the Offices de Tourisme (Tourist Offices) sell excellent "Guides Rando" (Hiking Guides), with plastic pages as protection against the weather, which list up to 50 hikes with the history of the area being hiked and details and maps of the hike itself on each page. We also hiked in the Principality of Andorra and skied at Baqueria Beret in Spain - a larger ski area than Vail in Colorado which is the largest in the USA.

Restaurant etiquette and protocol in France are second to none. Water (with no plastic straw) and bread are always provided without having to be asked for, specials are written out, no plate is taken away until all eaters have finished that course and the check ("l'addition") is never presented unless asked for - since presenting it unrequested is seen as a rude sign that the restaurant staff want the diners to leave. And there's little tipping as the wait staff are all paid a reasonable hourly wage - unlike in the USA where the restaurant pays the wait staff a pitiful hourly rate and then relies on the generosity of the customers to pay a large proportion of the staff's salaries in tips.

Most important of all is the fact that in France, and in many other countries, credit cards are never taken from a customer whether in restaurants or in stores. Instead, all wait staff in restaurants present an electronic bill/check to the customer in a small handheld computer where the credit card is inserted and the receipt printed out. None of the "I'll be right back" which often results in the card coming back up to 10 minutes later - sometimes with the card details having been copied down to be used for a fraudulent purchase online elsewhere. This scam has happened to me on a number of occasions in the USA and I've never understood why the same small computer is not used in the USA as it is in the majority of countries I've spent time in - including even in El Salvador. In addition to the chance of fraud, the US practice often involves wait staff standing in line to use the only restaurant computer which is counterproductive for the efficiency of the service..

Another French practice which impresses is the need to bring one's own eco-friendly bag to the supermarket since no paper or plastic bags are provided. And the small hand held plastic baskets in supermarkets also have four wheels and a telescopic vertical handle for ease of use and, if a large shopping cart is needed, a euro coin (currently about $1.40) is required to obtain a cart from a rack - the euro being refunded when the cart is returned. Supermarkets in the USA occasionally use a quarter to obtain a cart but who's going to return the cart for a mere 25 cents if it's raining or it's a distance to the rack? Hence, in France, no carts block parking spots or run down slopes and scratch a car as so often happens in the USA.

Road surfaces in southwest France are immaculately smooth and the lane discipline on the Autoroutes (Interstates) is second to none. Tolls on the Autoroutes are high but at least the fees are being used to keep the roads in tiptop condition with no pot holes and excellent signage.

One road we drove over many times had the sign "chaussee deformee" (meaning "uneven surface") and for the life of us we were unable to see what the sign was referring to. The smoothness of the roads put the majority of the roads in the USA to shame.

Speed control is maintained and speeding tickets on the Autoroutes are issued by mail with the use of hidden cameras. As a result, there are no gendarmes lurking by the side of the road attempting to increase their revenue through speeding tickets. Instead the officers are seen in villages and towns walking around while maintaining the peace and assisting residents with minor problems. Of course, there are no neon signs, no fire sirens, no traffic lights - only roundabouts - and no klaxons blasting away on fire trucks unless traffic is impeding progress. And very few billboards.

Having mentioned restaurant protocol, it would be remiss of me to not talk about the high quality and low cost of food and wine in supermarkets and in the restaurants themselves. Our local cafe, Cafe le Bayaa (the word Bayaa comes from the same family as the word Bayou in Louisiana) was a favorite watering hole and social gathering point and a glass of wine there cost the equivalent of $1.50. Salies has a wide variety of excellent restaurants with a three course meal rarely costing more than $20 and it has an excellent family run vineyard on the edge of town where the delicious rose, red and white wines sell for no more than $10 per bottle. The locals thought this was too expensive as the local supermarket, Carrefour, meaning Crossroad, sold good wines for approximately $3 per bottle.

To me, the most fascinating of the meals served are the "Menu Ouvriers" at a country auberge (inn) or relais (truck stop) - the latter being a far cry from our rather unattractive truck stops for drivers of long distance semis. "Menu Ouvrier" means Workers Menu and "routiers" (truck drivers) pull their "camions" (trucks) into the eating establishment promptly at noon for a five course meal, with no choice, of local "garbure" soup (cabbage, duck and ham), fish, steak, dessert and cheese - all for about $16 including a large flask of opened wine which is included in the price. Everyone sits at shared tables and imbibes a little wine and the routiers all wear their day glow pants for safety reasons when operating their behemoths. I was never aware of a case of routier DWI.

On the subject of day glow, all drivers in France are meant to carry two day glow vests in their car to be donned in the event of a breakdown so passing cars are made fully aware of the stationary car - especially if an occupant of the broken down car is changing a wheel on the driver's side in the right hand lane.

Upon leaving Salies after 10 months to return to Cranbury New Jersey, we held a "Soiree d'Adieu" (Goodbye Evening) for approximately 20 locals and, as mentioned earlier, when we returned to Salies, two years later, we held a "Soiree de Retour" (Return Evening).

What don't we like about life in La Belle France? My list of "likes" tops out at around 30 but there are a few practices which are not very appealing although most of these are fairly insignificant. Here are a few "dislikes":-

1)  Although "Canine Hygiene" boxes with bags are provided, dog poop is scattered on many sidewalks - especially in little alleyways.

2) Smoking in restaurants is not allowed but cigarette butts festoon the ground at outside cafes even though there are ash trays on the tables.

3) Bureaucracy at all levels - National, Regional, Local - is a nightmare and it took Lisa, being only an American Citizen, five months to obtain her "Carte de Sejour" (literally Card of Stay) from the Prefecture in Pau. A "Carte de Sejour" is required by all non-French citizens if they plan to stay in France longer than 90 days. Being a Dual Citizen, I was not required to go through this tedious process but for Lisa we had to produce Taxes (State and Federal), Birth Certificate, Wedding Certificate, Lease, Bank Statement etc, etc - all translated into French by an approved "traducteur" (translator) - and then to pay three visits to the Prefecture to finally obtain her Card. Our "traducteur", who was born in Wales but has lived all her adult life in France, has become a close friend and fellow rugby enthusiast as her father once played rugby for Wales.

4) Whereas the driving on Autoroutes and the driving in general and on the many roundabouts is excellent with headlights turned on in rainy or dull conditions and turn signals always used, the very close tailgating on narrow country lanes and in the mountains is downright scary. Reasons given are - a) we've always driven that way, b) it's easier to pass (not true) or c) it prevents another car getting between us and the one ahead. I'm sure the latter is the true answer.

It can be seen that we love rural France and its agreeable and tranquil lifestyle, the very friendly people, the gorgeous countryside and, of course, the cheap and delicious food and wine. And I did back France at long odds to win the World Cup football so I laughed all the way to the bank when I collected my winnings after Les Bleus were victorious.

I also do love the French rugby and, in particular, horse racing so there is not much I don't like about the country I first went to over 60 years ago. Having attended four French country weddings, flown with the French Navy's Aeronavale, hitchhiked and scootered around France, skied many times in the French Alps and having once visited the nearby Basque town of St Jean de Luz on the Atlantic 50 years ago, an arrow appeared to be pointing towards Salies de Bearn - a town that we had never heard of before but which is now near and dear to us in so many ways. We miss our many French friends in Salies and we hope that their lives are now back to normal after the appalling trauma of l'inondation.

# Chapter 20

## Tideswell in the Derbyshire Peak District

The exquisite unspoiled village of Tideswell lies in beautiful rolling countryside in the centre of the Derbyshire Peak District about a three hour drive north of London. Famous for its dry stone walls and plentiful sheep and some cows, the Peak District has many delightful villages and Tideswell sits about six miles from the two larger towns of Buxton and Bakewell. Buxton, an old spa town, claims to have the oldest hotel in England where a section of it dates back to 1573 and where Mary Queen of Scots was held in custody between 1576 and 1578. Bakewell is close to both the Haddon Hall and Chatsworth stately mansions and is famous for its sweet Bakewell Tart.

Tideswell, with its vast church known as "The Cathedral in the Peak" which dates back to the 1400s, sits at 1,000 feet above sea level with a current population of around 2,000 inhabitants. Settled many years ago due to the nearby lead mines (now long closed) and the cotton mills on the River Wye, Tidza, as the locals call it, is a magnificent example of preservation at its best. Many locals call themselves "Sawyeds"- a name which dates back to the story of a drunken farmer who was taking his cow to market when the cow got his head stuck in the bars of a wooden gate. Instead of attempting to extricate his cow, the farmer took the easier route and sawed off the cow's head.

Named after an Anglo Saxon chieftain called Tidi, Tideswell has every facility that a village needs - boasting three pubs, two first class restaurants, two cafes, two fish and chip shops, a butcher, a baker (but no candlestick

141

maker), a grocery, a pharmacy, a doctor and a fishmonger who comes to Tideswell in his van on a regular basis. And, of course, the village well. One 5 star restaurant, the Merchants Yard, started life as a business selling equipment to those in construction and was founded by a Polish gentleman in the late 1800s. It has now morphed into one of the finest restaurants to be found anywhere. One of the smaller cafes is named "High Nelly" after the old fashioned upright bicycle and it's a favorite eating place for the many cyclists who ride the Peak District enjoying the many hills and dales and looking for a simple place to have a bite to eat.

Not far away are several villages with their name ending in "low", which surprisingly means "hill" in old English, and one village, Foolow, was originally spelled the French "La Foulowe" meaning "The hill frequented by birds". Close by is Eyam - sadly famous for the Great Plague that hit this small village in 1666 resulting in the death of 260 villagers.

Lisa and I discovered the Peak District some years ago due to its wonderful hiking and have now been back each fall for a month at a time in the same tiny cottage that sits in Tideswell's market square near a very friendly pub called The Star.

Pub life in this part of England is very different from the standard American bar since the ancient pub is the social focal point of village life with excellent food, beer and wine and many events to draw in the customers in order to provide a convivial and fun atmosphere. Events such as Quiz, Darts, Backgammon and Checkers nights. And Sunday roast lunch is very popular and enjoyed by extended families of grandparents, parents and grandchildren since the majority of pubs are child and dog friendly. However unruly a dog may normally be, all dogs appear to have got the message about good table manners when they enter a pub and they lie silently underneath the table - of course hoping that fallen morsels will come their way.

Many pubs have delightful names going back many centuries - such as The Horse and Jockey, The Bull's Head, The Red Lion, The Pack Horse and even the Goat and Compasses whose name is derived from the religious saying "God encompasses us". Our favorite pub, The Barrel, in the tiny hamlet of Bretton with its five houses, sits at 1,300 feet and lays claim to being the highest pub in Derbyshire. Amazingly, five counties can be seen from the ridge on which The Barrel sits - Derbyshire, Cheshire, Lancashire, Staffordshire and South Yorkshire. A close second as to our favorite pub in the area is The

Red Lion in the next door village to Tideswell called Litton. Not only is the food and ambiance excellent and a quiz night regularly held but getting there can involve a spectacular walk across the fields which whets the appetite for The Red Lion's delicious food.

The Peak District itself has many hundreds of limestone dry stone walls with some having been there for nearly 300 years. These walls, which divide up the countryside into parcels of land, are the result of the many Enclosures Acts between 1600 and the early 1900s which were introduced by the monarchs to the detriment of the common farmer who, prior to these Acts, was able to graze his sheep and cows wherever he pleased. A majority of these walls were built in the mid 1800s and, although no cement was used in their construction, they have stood the test of time, criss-crossing the landscape and adding an appealing addition to the gorgeous countryside. Many of these walls have "Sheep-Creeps" - narrow slits in them which allow sheep to get through but not cows. Sheep far outnumber the cows but one of our favorite cows is the Belted Galloway - a black beast with a wide white belt running around the center of its torso.

A large area of the Peak District, as in most of Great Britain, is graced with the "Right to Roam" which allows walkers access to the majority of farmland and moors without the risk of trespassing. This wonderful ruling, which opens up so much of the countryside to those who love the outdoors, is very much the result of the "Great Trespass" of 1932. Until that time, the wealthy landowners had prevented public access in order to preserve their favorite shooting (hunting) grounds for the short period in the year when they were permitted to shoot grouse, pheasant, partridge and other game birds which had limited hunting seasons.

In 1932, as a protest, approximately 200 factory workers from the Manchester area descended on the Peak District and walked in a loop from the village of Hayfield up to the highest point called Kinder Scout to be greeted by police with many arrests being made. This brought attention to the restrictions imposed on the public by the wealthy landowners and a law was eventually enacted and so now the public have the right to ramble across some of the most beautiful countryside imaginable.

The Peak District is blessed with many wonderful vast and old stately mansions - a number of them now administered by the charitable National Trust - with Kedleston Hall, Lyme Park and Hardwick Hall being three of them. Another estate, Chatsworth, not a National Trust property, is the home of the Duke of Devonshire. The 11th Duke's wife Deborah, the Dowager Duchess known as "Debo', was the youngest of the intriguing six Mitford sisters - the oldest sister being Nancy who was a respected English author while another sister, Diana, was married to Sir Oswald Mosley, who was the leader of the British Union of Fascists prior to WWII. The Devonshire family also owned Bolsover Castle many years ago which they used as a playground to entertain royalty and their noble friends.

Another mansion, also not administered by the National Trust, is Haddon Hall whose original owners were the Vernon family who came to the shores of England with William the Conqueror in 1066. Another estate with Norman connections is Kedleston Hall whose original owners were the Curzons - Lord Curzon being the Viceroy of India in 1899.

All of these properties have vast estates with miles of hiking trails with one estate, Longshaw, having guided hikes on the nearby moors. And, not far from Tideswell, a ranger leads walks in the fall to spot the "rutting" red deer on the moors - which we did albeit at a distance.

A famous industrialist of the 1700s was Sir Richard Arkwright who invented spinning looms in Matlock Bath at the start of the Industrial Revolution and who also built the Cromford Canal – a commercial waterway, connected to the River Derwent, which was constructed to ship finished products to further south in England. We have taken a pleasant two hour ride in an original barge on the Cromford Canal with the barge being pulled along the towpath by a friendly horse named Ted.

One fall, we hiked over 50 miles covering such areas as Ilam, Dovedale, Mam Tor, Kinder and parts of the Pennine Way which starts nearby out of the village of Edale. We also hiked for three days on another part of the Pennine Way, further north in Cumbria, where this mostly north/south running trail then turns east/west and follows Hadrian's Wall which was built by the Roman Emperor Hadrian to keep out those dastardly Scots nearly 2,000 years ago. Edale had the last ski lift in England until it closed due to climate change in the 1960s and the village sits close to another unspoiled village - Castleton - which has some intriguing caves to explore. The Monsal Trail, - close by on the River Wye - is a "rails to trails" path on the old rail bed which connected Buxton to points further east.

A fun exercise is a historical treasure hunt to find a number of the standing stone circles which were erected by such as the Druids thousands of years ago. Using the very detailed Ordnance Survey maps, I've been able to discover the likes of Arbor Low, Nine Ladies and Doll Tor after struggling across the fields and into the woods to find these fascinating circles that pre-date the Roman occupation of England by many centuries. Very few folk make the effort to get to these circles and even locals that I asked for directional help were not aware of their existence or their locations.

Other spots to explore are the Potteries - with the factories of Wedgewood and Emma Bridgewater - not far south in Stoke on Trent in Staffordshire. And well worth a visit (and a hike) are the man-made reservoirs of "Dambuster" fame - Ladybower and Derwent - where Royal Air Force Lancaster bomber crews trained to drop the "bouncing bomb" which was used to destroy the German dams in the Ruhr Valley in WWII. The resultant flooding from the successful raids caused the destruction of much of the Nazi's war industry.

Above all, we love the friendship of the Tideswell locals and the compelling pub life with its games and contests - and the many social events that take place in the village. Such as the Harvest Supper in the Church Hall (with yet another Quiz) and the Tideswell version of London's "Last Night of the Proms" in the "Cathedral" which involves a surprising amount of Union Jack waving in a country not known for its displays of patriotism.

There are many characters in the village but two who stand out are the old boy who must be close to 100 who started work in a local cotton mill at the age of 14 and who now has one pint of local ale every day in The Red Lion in Litton and the other being elderly Ron who shows up at The Star at 9 pm each night, has two pints and then totters home. And a good friend, Tony, served in the Coldstream Guards and stood sentry duty outside the Queen's Buckingham Palace in London. Being from Derby, Tony is naturally a keen supporter of Derby County in the English Football League and he's enticed me to go and watch a home match with him when we are next back in town.

Not surprisingly, Tideswell has no neon, fluorescent or LED signs, no fire sirens and no overhead cables with preservation the number one priority for all the locals - many having lived in Tideswell all their life. So Tidza is now our English home away from home and we'll be back again to enjoy the hiking, the countryside, the National Trust houses, the pubs and the friendship and - and, of course, the Bakewell Tart and the Sticky Toffee Pudding!

Street in Tideswell in Derbyshire Peak District England

The Author on Hadrian's Wall England

Signs in French and Bearnais - Salies de Bearn

Old House in Salies de Bearn

Fete du Sel (Festival of Salt) Salies de Bearn

The Author with a T6 Texan aircraft

The Author with the Rev. Jesse Jackson

Crosswicks New Jersey Friends Quaker Meeting House

Syrian Children in Ritsona Camp in Greece